D0664006

Especially for

....

From

....

Date

....

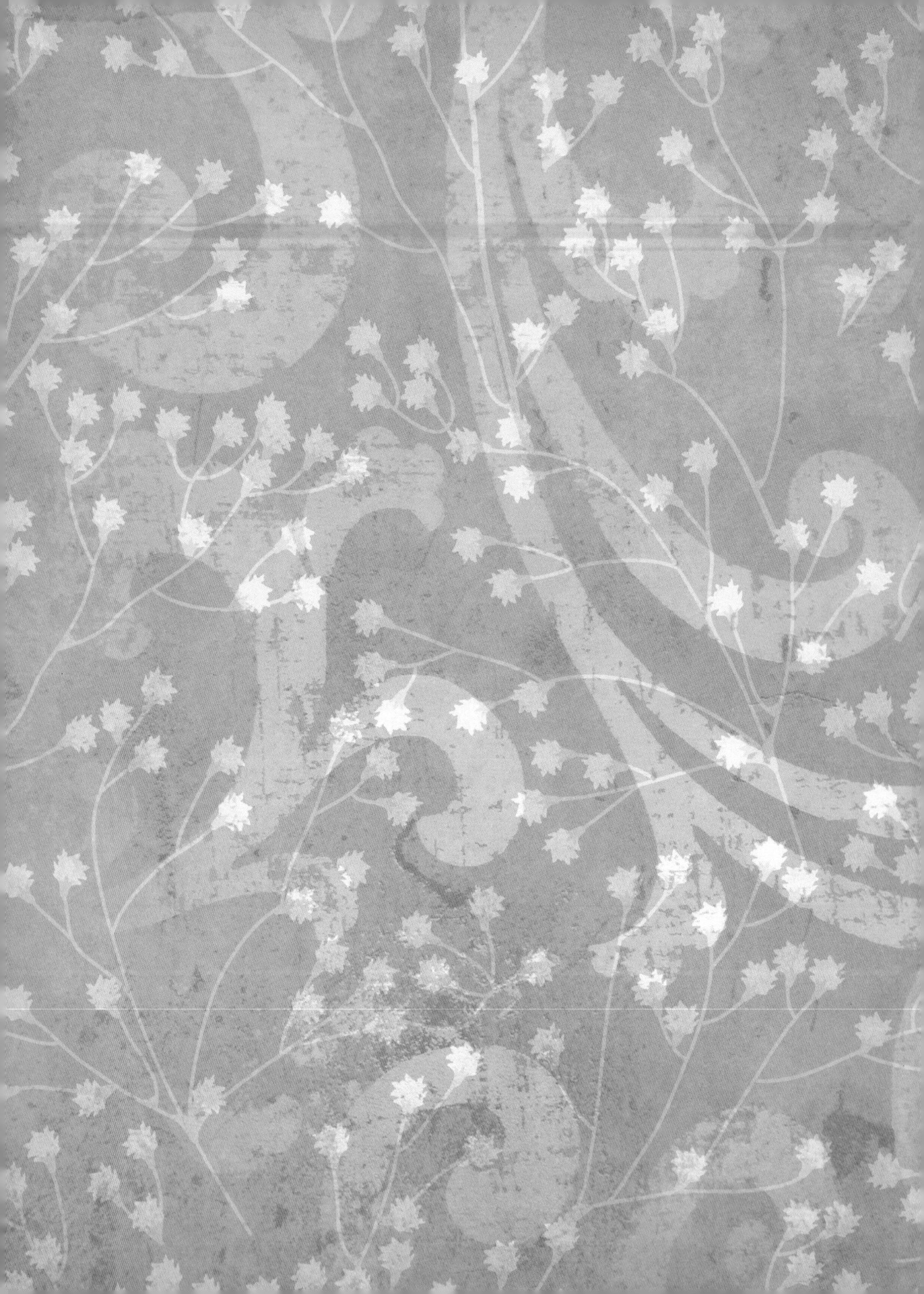

Daily Wisdom
for
Women
Morning & Evening
BARBOUR BOOKS
An Imprint of Barbour Publishing, Inc.

Compiled by Brigitta Nortker.

Print ISBN 978-1-63058-872-4

eBook Editions:

Adobe Digital Edition (.epub) 978-1-63409-419-1

Kindle and MobiPocket Edition (.prc) 978-1-63409-420-7

Devotional thoughts and prayers are from *Daily Wisdom for Women: 2013 Devotional Collection* and *Daily Whispers of Wisdom for Women* published by Barbour Publishing, Inc.

Published by Barbour Books, an imprint of Barbour Publishing, Inc., P.O. Box 719, Uhrichsville, Ohio 44683, www.barbourbooks.com

Our mission is to publish and distribute inspirational products offering exceptional value and biblical encouragement to the masses.

Printed in China.

Morning and Evening...
Wisdom for Your Soul

Evening, and morning. . .will I pray,
and cry aloud: and he shall hear my voice.
Psalm 55:17 KJV

. . . .

This lovely *Daily Wisdom for Women: Morning and Evening* edition will help you experience an intimate connection to the heavenly Father through a brief devotional thought, prayer, and scripture—twice a day for every day of the calendar year.

Enhance your spiritual journey with the refreshing readings and come to know just how deeply and tenderly God loves you.

Be blessed!

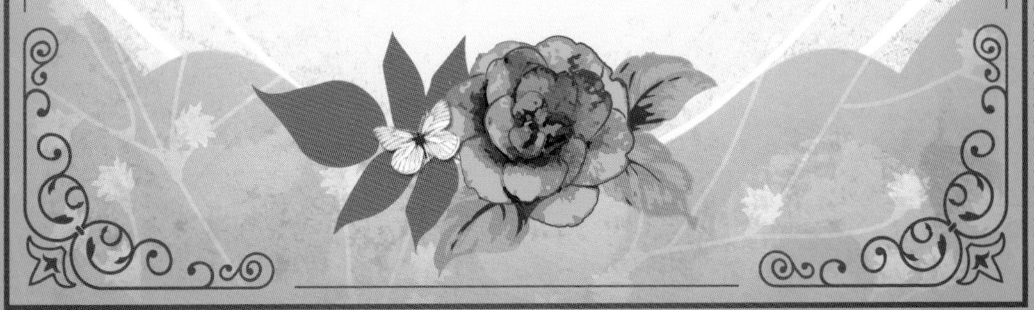

Morning

Created by God

So God created mankind in his own image, in the image of God he created them; male and female he created them.
Genesis 1:27 NIV

You are a woman; you were created in God's own image. He made you so He might have an ongoing relationship with you. You need Him, and He's promised to always be there for you. Now isn't that the kind of life companion you've searched for?

Lord, thank You for not only purposely creating me, but for loving me perfectly.

Evening

Rebirth

Create in me a clean heart, O God.
Renew a loyal spirit within me.
Psalm 51:10 NLT

God is always right there. . . . He is the Giver of life, the Renewer of hope, and He is ready and waiting to fill your soul with new life, new hope—to transform your heart and lift you out of the pit. All you have to do is ask.

Breath of life, breathe into me Your sweet joy and peace.
Help me to discard the old, embrace the new,
and fly on the wings of a dove.

DAY
2

Morning

David's Diary

God, God, save me! I'm in over my head, quicksand under me,
swamp water over me; I'm going down for the third time.
I'm hoarse from calling for help, bleary-eyed from searching the sky for God.
Psalm 69:1–3 msg

These ancient prayers remind us that nothing can shock God's ears. We can tell Him anything and everything. He won't forsake us—His love endures forever.

Oh Lord, You know the secrets of my family's hearts.
Teach us to talk to You through every emotion and every circumstance. Our focus belongs on You.

Evening

Sleeping Beauty

When you lie down, you will not be afraid;
when you lie down, your sleep will be sweet.
Proverbs 3:24 niv

You have a promise from the Bible that guarantees sweet sleep. Proverbs 3:24 says that you will not be afraid and that your sleep will be sweet. Isn't that good news? No more sleepless nights for you, sister!

God, I give all of my worries to You. Thanks for sweet sleep. Amen.

Morning

Needed: A Strong Spring

My voice shalt thou hear in the morning, O Lord; in the morning will I direct my prayer unto thee, and will look up.
Psalm 5:3 kjv

We need to begin our busy days on a strong spring. Not with just a good cup of coffee, but some time spent with our source of strength. No matter if we're facing wresting kids out of bed or fighting traffic all the way to work, that special time can give us a "spring in our step" today.

Thank You, Lord, for another day. Be my source of strength today. In Jesus' blessed name. Amen.

Evening

Ready to Catch You

God is our refuge and strength, an ever-present help in trouble.
Psalm 46:1 niv

Life can be unfair and painful and scary. Think of God. Reach out to Him. Run to Him like a little girl who runs to her daddy. God's shoulders are big enough to carry you, and His love is bright enough to fill those dark places with a light that is warm and safe and just right.

Jesus, let me feel Your presence, know Your love, and feel Your arms around me like a warm and cozy comforter. Amen.

DAY
4

MORNING

Joy in the Morning

All who seek the LORD will praise him.
Their hearts will rejoice with everlasting joy.
PSALM 22:26 NLT

In our own pain and frustration, there are times when our eyes don't see the beauty God sends. But if we'll ask, He'll show us. God is faithful to build us up with everything we need to serve Him with joy. What an awesome God we serve!

Lord God, I thank You for Your joy; I thank You for providing it every day to sustain me. I will be joyful in You.

EVENING

Follow Your Creator

You created every part of me; you put me together in my mother's womb.
PSALM 139:13 GNT

We have a Creator whom we can identify with. God made each of us unique, but we have the ability to know who He is and to recognize Him if we get lost. We have a special relationship with Him because He made us in His image. He wants us to recognize and follow Him.

Dear Father, I know You created me and have given me signs that point to You. I will follow You because You know exactly what I need. Amen.

MORNING

Renewal of All Things

"Truly I say to you, that you who have followed Me, in the regeneration when the Son of Man will sit on His glorious throne, you also shall sit upon twelve thrones, judging the twelve tribes of Israel."
MATTHEW 19:28 NASB

None of us will just occupy space in heaven. Our God is always productive. And this job to which Jesus refers, that of judging the twelve tribes of Israel, will be given to the disciples.

Lord, I can't even imagine what You have in store for me in heaven. Please keep me faithful to complete the duties You've called me to on earth.

EVENING

Every Day's a Holiday

"But seek first the kingdom of God and his righteousness, and all these things will be added to you."
MATTHEW 6:33 ESV

God knows exactly what to give you because He knows what you need better than anyone else. What God has to give is the best quality, and it won't ever break or go out of style. And His gifts are free and totally undeserved. You can celebrate God's good gifts all year round!

God, on days when I feel like nothing is going my way, help me to remember all the things You've given me and all the ways You take care of me. Amen.

DAY
6

Morning

He Enjoys You

"The Lord your God is in your midst, a mighty one who will save; he will rejoice over you with gladness."
Zephaniah 3:17 ESV

Our mighty Savior offers us a personal relationship, loving and rejoicing over us, His children, glad that we live and move in Him. He is the Lord of the universe, and yet He will quiet our restless hearts and minds with His tender love.

Lord, help me remember that You are always with me and that You delight in me. Remind me that I am Your child and that You enjoy our relationship.

Evening

It's Not about Stuff

"For everyone who asks receives, and the one who seeks finds, and to the one who knocks it will be opened."
Matthew 7:8 ESV

This verse isn't talking about "stuff"—material things that everyone else is getting. Nope. It's definitely not about that. God *does* promise to take care of *all* our needs, but this verse is about seeking after God and wanting what He wants for you.

Dear God, help me not to be consumed with "stuff." I want to seek after You, and I trust You to take care of all my needs. Amen.

Morning

Perfect Peace and Rest

For thus said the Lord God, the Holy One of Israel, "In returning and rest you shall be saved; in quietness and in trust shall be your strength." But you were unwilling.
Isaiah 30:15 ESV

Frances Ridley Havergal's devotion to God throughout her short life is seen in her many hymns. The nineteenth-century Englishwoman's life was riddled with pain and sickness, yet she sought the Lord through it all.

Father, I'm tired of trying to outrun my problems. May Your peace flow through me like a mighty river, bringing rest to my soul.

Evening

God's Word Is Light

Your word is a lamp that gives light wherever I walk.
Psalm 119:105 CEV

Just like trying to walk through a dark house, many people are stumbling through life. They have not discovered the truths of God's Word. Wherever we go and whatever we do, we can rely on God's Word to guide us. Even in unfamiliar places or at difficult crossroads, you don't have to be afraid or confused.

God, thank You for the light You have provided through Your Holy Word. Teach me as I read my Bible. Amen.

DAY
8

Morning

Seeking Wisdom

And a man of understanding will acquire wise counsel,
to understand a proverb and a figure,
the words of the wise and their riddles.
PROVERBS 1:5–6 NASB

Satan may be out of the garden, but he still finds his way into vulnerable areas of our lives. But God is with you, even in times of sinful temptation. He's promised to give you the power to withstand such moral crises.

Lord, surround me with friends who know You and Your Word.
Surround me in a crisis so I can still hear Your voice of wisdom and reason.

Evening

Clueless

"The grass withers, the flower fades,
but the word of our God stands forever."
ISAIAH 40:8 NKJV

Without the Bible, we would be clueless. We wouldn't have the confidence to make good decisions. We wouldn't feel God's love and blessings because we wouldn't be able to recognize what they are. We wouldn't pray for help if we couldn't read about the amazing ways He has helped others. The bottom line? . . . God's Word gives us the answers we need.

God, I promise to read Your Book as often as I can. Amen.

Morning

Sweet Aroma

The heartfelt counsel of a friend is as sweet as perfume and incense.
Proverbs 27:9 NLT

Friendships that have Christ as their center are wonderful relationships blessed by the Father. Through the timely, godly advice these friends offer, God speaks to us, showering us with comfort that is as sweet as perfume and incense. So what are you waiting for? Make a date with a friend and share the sweet aroma of Jesus!

Jesus, Your friendship means the world to me.
I value the close friendships You've blessed me with, too!

Evening

What God Wants

He has shown you, O man, what is good; and what does the Lord require of you but to do justly, to love mercy, and to walk humbly with your God?
Micah 6:8 NKJV

Starting at this very moment, and every moment for the rest of our lives, God wants us to show compassion and mercy. He wants us to stand up for what is right and good. And He wants us to love Him with all our hearts.

Dear Father, thank You for showing me what You want me to do.
Help me to always do the right thing. Amen.

DAY
10

Morning

Full of Grace

Let your conversation be always full of grace, seasoned with salt, so that you may know how to answer everyone.
Colossians 4:6 niv

When our conversations are full of grace, people will enjoy communicating with us. They will walk away blessed by the love we have shown. Today, in your conversations, extend God's grace to those hungry to experience His love.

Dear Lord, may I view each conversation as an opportunity to extend Your grace to others. May my words be a blessing. Amen.

Evening

Jehovah Jireh—Your Provider

I was young and now I am old, yet I have never seen the righteous forsaken or their children begging bread.
Psalm 37:25 niv

The Bible is full of promises. But that doesn't mean God is some kind of magic genie who gives you everything you want. Putting God first will satisfy you in every way. And that's a promise the world can't make or keep.

Dear God, thank You for being my Provider. Give me a heart that follows after You so that I won't become focused on the things of this world.

MORNING

Keeping a Clean Heart

Therefore, having these promises, beloved, let us cleanse ourselves from all filthiness of the flesh and spirit, perfecting holiness in the fear of God.
2 CORINTHIANS 7:1 NKJV

Keeping a clean heart requires similar diligence and regular upkeep. While Jesus Himself cleanses us from all unrighteousness, as believers we need to be on the lookout for temptations and situations that might cause us to fall into sin in the first place.

"Create in me a clean heart, O God, and renew a steadfast spirit within me" (Psalm 51:10 NKJV). Amen.

EVENING

Quiet Time with God

Be still, and know that I am God; I will be exalted among the nations, I will be exalted in the earth!
PSALM 46:10 NKJV

Pray; pour your heart out to Him. And when you say, "amen," don't rush away. Be still and listen. You just might be surprised at how God makes His presence known to you. The Creator wants you to be still and fully know that He is God, and He will guide you through every step of every day.

Dear God, please help me to be patient and listen for Your guidance instead of rushing off to do what I want to do. Amen.

DAY 12

Morning

He Keeps His Promises

"For I know the plans I have for you," declares the LORD,
"plans to prosper you and not to harm you,
plans to give you hope and a future."
JEREMIAH 29:11 NIV

We can always trust the words of our Lord. He knows the plans He has for us, and He has the power to see them through. Hope and a future, prosperity and peace—we can trust that, even when things seem hopeless, God is still at work, carrying out His promises.

Thank You for having a perfect plan and for keeping Your promises. Give me faith to believe in You even when it seems like everything is going wrong.

Evening

I've Got the Joy!

When anxiety was great within me, your consolation brought me joy.
PSALM 94:19 NIV

Isn't it awesome to think that the God of the universe loves you? That He knows everything about you? He knows that life here on earth isn't easy. He understands the trials and hardships you go through. And He's longing for you to reach out and grab onto His joy, which cannot be taken away. No matter what.

God, thank You for being with me each and every day.
Thank You for Your joy.

Morning

Trials Have a Purpose

"I am your brother Joseph, whom you sold into Egypt. And now do not be grieved or angry with yourselves, because you sold me here; for God sent me before you to preserve life."
GENESIS 45:4–5 NASB

Joseph walked through his humiliating ordeal with his eyes focused on the Lord. He continued not only to love his brothers but to find forgiveness in his heart for them. Studying his life can enable us to look at our own situations differently: God can accomplish miracles in the midst of trials.

Lord, sometimes I want to enjoy my agony awhile longer. Show me the brilliance of Your forgiveness that I might trust You in the trial and not miss the outcome You've planned.

Evening

Just What I Need!

"And you, my son Solomon, acknowledge the God of your father, and serve him with wholehearted devotion and with a willing mind, for the LORD searches every heart and understands every desire and every thought."
1 CHRONICLES 28:9 NIV

Ever felt like no one else knows what you're going through? Ever feel so alone that you give up hope? When these times come, remember, God understands every single emotion you feel and He is ready and waiting to encourage you.

Oh God, I'm so thankful for Your love and encouragement. Help me to never forget that You understand me.

DAY 14

Morning

A Prosperous Soul

Beloved, I wish above all things that thou mayest prosper and be in health, even as thy soul prospereth.
3 John 1:2 KJV

Today's scripture is so encouraging. God wants us to prosper and He loves for us to be in good health, even as our souls prosper. If we really think about that, we have to conclude that the health of our soul is even more important than our physical health. Spend some time today giving your soul a workout.

Today I draw near to You. Make me healthy. . .from the inside out.

Evening

A Teddy Bear Hug

I was very worried, but you comforted me and made me happy.
Psalm 94:19 NCV

Did you know that God gives hugs? It's true! When your heart is hurting, you can reach out to Him and He will pull you into His arms, giving you a spiritual squeeze, guaranteed to help you forget about your sadness. He's right there, ready to comfort you and wipe away your tears.

Lord, thank You for caring so much about me! When I'm going through hard times, You love me so much that You give me spiritual hugs. I need those, and I'm so grateful! Amen.

MORNING

Self-Examination

Let us test and examine our ways, and return to the LORD!
LAMENTATIONS 3:40 ESV

As we set aside time for solitude and reflection, the Holy Spirit will gently show us these things if we ask. He will show us the sins we need to confess and give us the grace of repentance. Experiencing forgiveness, our fellowship with our heavenly Father is restored.

Lord, speak to me through Your Holy Spirit of what is wrong in my life. Give me the gift of repentance and allow me to enjoy the sweetness of Your forgiveness.

EVENING

Just Do It!

But don't just listen to God's word. You must do what it says. Otherwise, you are only fooling yourselves.
JAMES 1:22 NLT

"Actions speak louder than words" is a true and common phrase used to help people understand the idea of letting your beliefs or words show through your actions. It's wonderful to hide God's Word in your heart, but if it isn't changing you. . .if you aren't actively doing something about it. . . your faith won't seem very important.

God, please help me to talk less and do more.

DAY
16

Morning

The New Me

Therefore, if anyone is in Christ, the new creation has come:
The old has gone, the new is here!
2 Corinthians 5:17 niv

Since God Himself sees us as a new creation, how can we do any less? We need to choose to see ourselves as a new creation, too. And we can, through God's grace.

If you are "in Christ," you are a new creation. Be glad. Give thanks. Live each day as the new creation you have become through Jesus.

Please give me the spiritual eyes to see myself as a new creation,
looking past the guilt of yesterday's choices.

Evening

Waiting with Hope

Blessed are all who wait for him!
Isaiah 30:18 niv

If God has promised you something, and you believe that He keeps His promises, you will have hope. You will have hope because you know that something good is going to happen—in God's time, in God's way.

Lord Jesus, sometimes it's really hard to wait for what I want.
But please help me to trust You and wait for Your plans for my life with hope.

Morning

A Refuge from Our Despair

Let me dwell in Your tent forever;
let me take refuge in the shelter of Your wings.
Psalm 61:4 NASB

King David, writer of this psalm, composed it as a song, acknowledging God as his Rock. He clung with tenacity to the fact that no matter how desperate his situation appeared, God was as immovable as a huge rock or boulder. Although David's trials may differ from yours, you, too, can use strong coping mechanisms.

Lord, I search for a way through the torrents of despair.
How precious is the knowledge that You hear and care.

Evening

Bless the Lord!

Let every thing that hath breath praise the Lord.
Psalm 150:6 KJV

Thank God for the birds, trees, sunshine, and clouds. Thank Him for blessing you with talents and for giving you a bright, healthy mind. Thank Him for keeping His promise of providing everything you need. And most of all, thank Him for sending a Savior to die for your sins so that you can have eternal life.

Lord, thank You for loving me and supplying all my needs.
Thank You for showering me with more blessings than I could ever count.

DAY 18

Morning

Make a Choice

Do not let your hearts be troubled (distressed, agitated). You believe in and adhere to and trust in and rely on God; believe in and adhere to and trust in and rely also on Me.
John 14:1 amp

Some days are full of joy and peace; others are not. When we face the inevitable dark days in life, we must choose how we respond. We bring light to the darkest of days when we turn our face to God. Rely on Him to lead you through the darkest days.

Oh Lord, still my troubled heart. Let me learn to rely on You in all circumstances. Thank You, Father, for Your everlasting love.

Evening

God Knows My Thoughts

You know when I am resting or when I am working, and from heaven you discover my thoughts.
Psalm 139:2 cev

Nothing brings God greater joy than when one of His children chooses to spend time with Him. Talk to God throughout your day today. Understand that He is constantly with you. You can even say a prayer inside your mind. No matter how you pray, He hears!

Thank You, Lord, for always being present. You know me, and You love me no matter where I am or what I am doing. Amen.

Morning

His Perfect Strength

"My grace is sufficient for you, for my power is made perfect in weakness." Therefore I will boast all the more gladly about my weaknesses, so that Christ's power may rest on me.
2 Corinthians 12:9 NIV

In an uncertain world, it is difficult to say few things for sure. But no matter what life throws our way, we can be confident of this: our demands will *never* exceed God's vast resources.

Strong and mighty heavenly Father, thank You that in my weakness I can always rely on Your perfect strength. Amen.

Evening

Plant the Seeds of Joy

Clap your hands for joy, all peoples!
Praise God with loud songs!
Psalm 47:1 GNT

God loves to hear our praises, and He sends us joy when we show Him our love and gratitude. When you are filled with this fruit, others will see and want what you have. Think of what a better world it would be if we all shared this kind of joy.

Heavenly Father, thank You for giving me the fruit of joy. I will praise You even when things aren't going well. Amen.

DAY
20

Morning

Wisdom Calls Out

"For wisdom is better than jewels;
and all desirable things cannot compare with her."
Proverbs 8:11 NASB

Wisdom calls to all of us, but some of us are just better listeners. Notice that earlier in this passage that wisdom is found "on top of the heights beside the way, where the paths meet" (Proverbs 8:2 NASB). Wisdom is a choice. We can walk right past it.

Lord, You lay before me a path of righteousness.
Please help me desire to walk with You!

Evening

My Treasured Delight

Your Word I have treasured in my heart,
that I may not sin against You.
Psalm 119:11 NASB

God has given you His Word to study, delight in, treasure, and apply. His grace is overflowing and abounding. . . . Thank Him, beloved. He's poured out His life, His love, and His Word for *you*.

Father, thank You for Your Word.
Thank You that everything I ever need is right there.

Morning

Unchained!

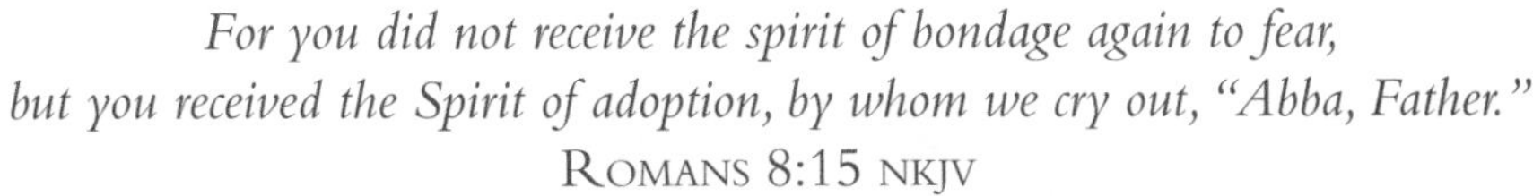

*For you did not receive the spirit of bondage again to fear,
but you received the Spirit of adoption, by whom we cry out, "Abba, Father."*
Romans 8:15 NKJV

Do you struggle with fear? Do you feel it binding you with its invisible chains? If so, then there's good news. Through Jesus, you have received the Spirit of adoption. A daughter of the Most High God has nothing to fear. Today, acknowledge your fears to the Lord. He will loose your chains and set you free.

*Lord, thank You that I don't have to live in fear.
I am Your child, Your daughter, and You are my Daddy-God!*

Evening

Practical Wisdom

Then you will understand what is right and just and fair—every good path.
Proverbs 2:9 NIV

Sometimes you can watch something start to unfold and realize it isn't for you. God depends on you to use the wisdom He gave you to figure out whether to stay and participate or get out of a situation. Practicing this kind of wisdom doesn't always feel good, but God trusts you to act on His behalf. He's working through you.

*God, I want to be Your hero. Help me to respond to You,
no matter what people might think. Amen.*

DAY 22

Morning

Don't Give In

You are famous, God, for welcoming God-seekers,
for decking us out in delight.
Psalm 5:12 MSG

When we have those down-in-the-dumps days, we should encircle ourselves with encouragers, Christian friends who can hold up our arms, like Moses, when we're unable to continue the journey. We can reach for God's Word, which breathes life into our spirits. Moments of prayer will connect us to the Life-Giver and refresh us.

Heavenly Father, I lift my eyes to the heavens and ask for Your peace. Thank You for Your love and care. Thank You for standing by my side. I praise Your name.

Evening

The Word of Truth

But his delight is in the law of the Lord,
and in His law he meditates day and night.
Psalm 1:2 NASB

Memorizing God's Word is one of the best things you can do. That's "accurately handling the word of truth" (2 Timothy 2:15 NASB). Do you think God meant for His Word to be read then forgotten? Use the magnificent weapon He's supplied by dwelling on it!

Lord, please help me to study and memorize Your Word continually, faithfully, diligently. I love You, Father. In Jesus' name I pray. Amen.

MORNING

Lay It at the Cross

*"Come to me, all you who are weary and burdened,
and I will give you rest."*
MATTHEW 11:28 NIV

Do you have any difficulties in life, any burdens, worries, fears, relationship issues, financial troubles, or work problems that you need to "lay at the cross"? Jesus says, "Come."

Lord, thank You for inviting me to come and exchange my heavy burden for Your light burden. I praise You for the rest You promise me. Amen.

EVENING

Do You Know His Voice?

*"My sheep listen to my voice;
I know them, and they follow me."*
JOHN 10:27 NIV

Sometimes you'll have a thought and you'll wonder, *Was that me, or was that God?* If your thought is in line with the Bible, it's probably God. If it doesn't line up with God's Word, then it couldn't have been His voice. Listen carefully. . .He is worth hearing.

*God, please help me to know Your voice,
and help me to always follow You. Amen.*

MORNING

I Am a Friend of God

When Jesus saw their faith, he said,
"Friend, your sins are forgiven."
LUKE 5:20 NIV

Isn't it amazing to realize God calls us His friend? He reaches out to us with a friendship that goes above and beyond the very best the world has to offer. Best of all, He's not the sort of friend who loses touch or forgets to call. He's always there.

Oh Lord, I'm so blessed to be called Your friend! You're the best one I'll ever have. Thank You for the kind of friendship that supersedes all boundaries.

EVENING

Road Map

Your word is a lamp for my feet,
a light on my path.
PSALM 119:105 NIV

God's Word helps us know the right things! When we're not sure which way to go or how to handle a certain situation, the Bible serves as a road map to guide us. The more we read it, the more confident we can be that we're taking the right path.

Dear Father, thank You for Your Word.
Help me to read it and understand it.

Morning

A Woman of Folly

The woman of folly is boisterous, she is naive and knows nothing.
PROVERBS 9:13 NASB

Have you ever felt like this woman? Did you start out with endless options and then begin purchasing tickets to oblivion? With Christ it's not too late to cash in that pass to nowhere. With Christ your life will have direction.

Lord, please provide me with a true picture of myself.
Guide me to the place You envision for me.

Evening

An Answer That Is Always "Yes!"

If we [freely] admit that we have sinned and confess our sins, He is faithful and just (true to His own nature and promises) and will forgive our sins [dismiss our lawlessness] and [continuously] cleanse us from all unrighteousness [everything not in conformity to His will in purpose, thought, and action].
1 JOHN 1:9 AMP

Because Jesus died for all of us, His answer to our request is always yes! He is faithful to forgive our sins.

Dear Father, thank You for forgiving me and for not having a limit on how many times You'll do that. Please help me to remember to say I'm sorry each time I sin. Amen.

DAY 26

Morning

Shining Light

"You are the light of the world.
A town built on a hill cannot be hidden."
Matthew 5:14 NIV

Being a light of the world is not about being a Bible thumper or bashing others over the head with religion. It's about living out genuine faith that allows Christ's light to break through our everyday lives. With that goal in mind, shine!

Jesus, You are my true light. Even though I alone can't shine as brightly as You, I ask that You shine through me as I seek to follow after You.

Evening

Don't Conform, Transform!

And so, dear brothers and sisters, I plead with you to give your bodies to God because of all he has done for you. Let them be a living and holy sacrifice—the kind he will find acceptable. This is truly the way to worship him.
Romans 12:1 NLT

As followers of Jesus, God wants you to do what you know in your heart is right—no matter what everyone else is doing. Be true to the heavenly Creator, and follow His leading in your heart. Ask Him to transform your thoughts to be good and pleasing to Him.

Dear God, please transform my thoughts to match Your thoughts. Amen.

MORNING

Lead Goose

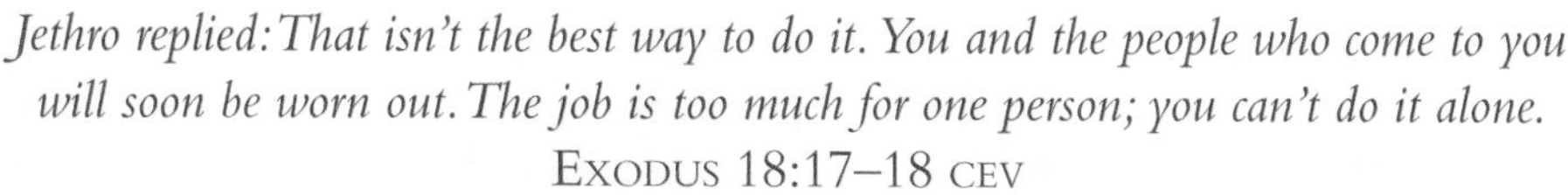

Jethro replied: That isn't the best way to do it. You and the people who come to you will soon be worn out. The job is too much for one person; you can't do it alone.
EXODUS 18:17–18 CEV

We often find ourselves as a lead goose. We have a hard time recognizing signs of exhaustion in ourselves. Even harder is falling back and letting someone else have a chance to develop leadership skills.

Dear Lord, help me to know when to fall back and rest, letting someone else take the lead. Teach me to serve You in any position. Amen.

EVENING

Freedom

It was for freedom that Christ set us free; therefore keep standing firm and do not be subject again to a yoke of slavery.
GALATIANS 5:1 NASB

Christ set you free so that you would live in *His everlasting freedom*. He doesn't want you to turn back to the worthless and sinful things of this world. He wants you to live in His pure and gracious freedom!

Lord, thank You for freedom. Please help me to live freely and not be under "a yoke of slavery." In Jesus' name I pray, amen.

DAY
28

MORNING

Voice of the Shepherd

"My sheep listen to my voice; I know them, and they follow me."
JOHN 10:27 NIV

God's voice is distinct—and when we become part of His family, we learn to recognize it. The more we tune in to that distinct voice, the more we'll hear it. Let's be like a child, eager to hear a parent's loving voice.

Lord, please give me ears to hear Your still, small voice, and the strength and faith to obey what You say to me.

EVENING

The Bible Will Guide Me

Jesus commented, "Even more blessed are those who hear God's Word and guard it with their lives!"
LUKE 11:28 MSG

You have the Bible, God's Word! There is no other book that can help you live the life God has called you to live. Its pages hold everything you will ever need to know in this life. God has a plan for us, and if we stay in His Word and read it often, He will speak to us through it and show us the way to go. Guard it. Appreciate it. Love it.

Dear God, thank You for providing guidance through the scriptures.

Morning

Forsaken by God?

*My God, my God, why have You forsaken me?
Far from my deliverance are the words of my groaning.*
Psalm 22:1 nasb

Have you ever cried out to God with such despairing utterances as these? Jesus, separated from the Father because of our sin, reached the ear of God with His own desperation. He experienced for us this ultimate terror. . .that we would never be forsaken or walk alone the road that leads to Calvary.

Lord, no matter what hazards are down the road, You have a signpost ready to hang on whatever misleading marker is already in the ground. And the Son is shining ahead!

Evening

You Are God's Best Work

For you created my inmost being; you knit me together in my mother's womb. I praise you because I am fearfully and wonderfully made; your works are wonderful, I know that full well.
Psalm 139:13–14 niv

You are exactly the person God planned you to be. You are His workmanship. On the day you chose Him as your Lord, you melted His heart. There is nothing He wouldn't do for you, because He's crazy about you!

Dear God, thank You for making me who I am and loving me no matter what. Amen.

DAY 30

Morning

Holy Spirit Prayers

We do not know how to pray as we should,
but the Spirit Himself intercedes for us with
groanings too deep for words.
Romans 8:26 NASB

We can be encouraged, knowing that our deepest longings and desires, maybe unknown even to us, are presented before the God who knows us and loves us completely. Our names are engraved on His heart and hands. He never forgets us; He intervenes in all things for our good and His glory.

Father, I thank You for the encouragement these verses bring.
May I always be aware of the Holy Spirit's interceding on my behalf.

Evening

A Natural Beauty

Cultivate inner beauty, the gentle,
gracious kind that God delights in.
1 Peter 3:4 MSG

It's so easy to get distracted by the magazines and commercials constantly telling us that we're not enough. Not thin enough. Not stylish enough. Whenever you feel completely lacking, remember that natural beauty comes from within and shines outward.

Lord, I know You think I'm beautiful just the way
You created me; help me to see that as well. Amen.

MORNING

Giver of Good Things

For the LORD God is a sun and shield; the LORD will give grace and glory; no good thing will He withhold from those who walk uprightly.
PSALM 84:11 NKJV

Worry is such a useless practice, like spinning wheels on a vehicle that takes you nowhere. And yet we women are notorious for it. The Bible advises us to let each day take care of itself. We are promised that God will provide for us.

Father, give me patience, and help me to see the good gifts from You in each day—even the small ones. Amen.

EVENING

The Master of You-ology

But the very hairs of your head are all numbered.
MATTHEW 10:30 KJV

Why do you react to certain things the way you do? What is it about that particular person that gets on your nerves? The answer is clear to God. Best of all, He knows how to change you. If you have attitudes that need adjusting (and who doesn't?), God has all the right tools for tweaking.

Lord, give me the desire to change when I need to so that I become more and more like You. Amen.

DAY 32

Morning

People Pleaser versus God Pleaser

We are not trying to please people but God,
who tests our hearts.
1 Thessalonians 2:4 niv

It is impossible to please both God and man. We must make a choice. Man looks at the outward appearance, but God looks at the heart. Align your heart with His. Let go of impression management that focuses on outward appearance. Receive God's unconditional love and enjoy the freedom to be yourself before Him!

Dear Lord, may I live for You alone.
Help me transition from a people
pleaser to a God pleaser. Amen.

Evening

Do You Know God's Will?

Each of you should use whatever gift you have received to serve others,
as faithful stewards of God's grace in its various forms.
1 Peter 4:10 niv

As a Christian, in addition to talents, you also have spiritual gifts. God wants you to use your gifts and abilities for His glory. When you do, you are fulfilling His will for your life. His plan for you will always match up with the things you do well!

God, please reveal to me my unique gifts and abilities.
May I always use them for Your glory. Amen.

MORNING

To Touch Jesus' Cloak

And a woman who had a hemorrhage for twelve years, and had endured much at the hands of many physicians, and had spent all that she had and was not helped at all, but rather had grown worse—after hearing about Jesus, she came up in the crowd behind Him and touched His cloak. For she thought, "If I just touch His garments, I will get well."
MARK 5:25–28 NASB

She's been miraculously healed and now she demonstrates her faith by worshipping at Jesus' feet. Does your faith shine through even in small gestures?

Lord, You heal me when I come to You, by renewing my spirit and deepening my faith. I worship Your majesty and power.

EVENING

Need Wisdom?

If you need wisdom, ask our generous God, and he will give it to you.
JAMES 1:5 NLT

If we want wisdom, we have to look to God and ask Him to give it to us. And when you do ask God for wisdom, never doubt that He will grant it. Trust that He will give you all the wisdom you need to accomplish the plans that He has for you—at just the right time.

Dear God, I definitely need a lot of wisdom. Help me to trust You more. Amen.

DAY
34

Morning

A New Name

"And I will give to each one a white stone, and on the stone will be engraved a new name that no one understands except the one who receives it."
REVELATION 2:17 NLT

God will give each of His children a new name, reflecting something unique and special in our lives. God looks into our inmost being and gives us a name that carries the essence of our new creation in Christ.

What might your new name be?

Dear Lord, I look forward to the day when I will receive my new name, one that reflects the very essence of who I am in You.

Evening

God's Love Is My Support

When I said, "My foot is slipping,"
your unfailing love, LORD, supported me.
PSALM 94:18 NIV

God's love is greater than anything you or I could ever dream of—it's deeper than the deepest ocean, wider than the span of the earth, and bigger than the universe itself. And on days when you feel alone, His love will support you. Even if the earth crumbled around you, His love would still be there.

Jesus, thank You for never leaving me. Thank You for dying for me so that I might live.

DAY 35

MORNING

The Great Gift Giver

Every good and perfect gift is from above, coming down from the Father of the heavenly lights, who does not change like shifting shadows.
JAMES 1:17 NIV

God is a gift giver. He is, in fact, the Creator of all good gifts. He finds great joy in blessing you. The God who made you certainly knows you by name. He even knows your favorites and your dreams. Most important, God knows your needs.

God, sometimes I am anxious. I want what I want, and I want it now. Calm my spirit and give me the patience to wait for Your perfect gifts. Amen.

EVENING

Chase Comfort

The LORD is close to the brokenhearted; he rescues those whose spirits are crushed.
PSALM 34:18 NLT

As Christians, we need to be still and let the truth of God wash over our hurts. Even though stillness is quiet and physically inactive, it is an intentional action that pursues God's peace. Today, quiet your busy mind, and let the peace of God soothe all your hurts.

Father, I cry before You and wait for Your perfect peace to wash over my pain and heal my heart. Please comfort me in my sorrow. Amen.

DAY
36

Morning

An Extravagant God

Come back to God, your God. And here's why:
God is kind and merciful. He takes a deep breath, puts up with a lot,
this most patient God, extravagant in love.
Joel 2:13 MSG

Focusing on the negative—choosing despair—doesn't bring life. Voluntarily focusing on Jesus will. Praise Him for all your blessings: they are there; look for them! Some might be tiny, others magnificent. But they're all because of our Lord Jesus Christ. He is a most patient God and extravagant in His love.

Heavenly Father, I praise Your name. You are extravagant in our love,
filling me to overflowing! I am grateful for all You've done.

Evening

The Dream Giver

For we are God's masterpiece. He has created us anew in Christ Jesus,
so we can do the good things he planned for us long ago.
Ephesians 2:10 NLT

Our dreams are part of who we are, but sometimes we're afraid to think we could do something big. It may take awhile, but if we believe God wants our dreams to come true, we just need to wait for Him to open the doors to make them happen.

Dear God, I want to explore the dreams You have put in my heart.
Help me to see the way I should go.

Morning

Jesus Is Tempted by Satan

And the devil said to Him, "If You are the Son of God, tell this stone to become bread." And Jesus answered him, "It is written, 'Man shall not live on bread alone.' "
Luke 4:3–4 NASB

Have you ever found yourself so tempted to sin that you ached all the way to your soul? Christ understands that pull toward evil. Satan wasn't just present in the wilderness to "bug" the Lord Jesus Christ. This was a full-on frontal attack. And the stakes were high. For if Christ succumbed to Satan's snare, He would be ineligible to make that perfect sacrifice on the cross as the Lamb of God without blemish.

Lord, I thank You for Your Son's perfect victory over Satan.

Evening

Only a Phone Call Away

Pray without ceasing.
1 Thessalonians 5:17 ESV

Imagine God has His ear pressed to the phone on the other end of the line, wanting to listen and desiring a connection with you. A prayer can be a simple and sincere "Help me" or a long monologue about a frustrating day. Even if your mind wanders or you're half asleep, God will still be on the other end of the line, listening to your prayer.

Father, thank You for always listening. I invite You to be a part of my life as my constant companion. Amen.

DAY 38

Morning

Hurt by Others' Choices

God heard the boy crying. The angel of God called from Heaven to Hagar, "What's wrong, Hagar? Don't be afraid. God has heard the boy and knows the fix he's in."
Genesis 21:17 MSG

God is always on our side when we suffer because of others' choices. Even when we have lost hope, God's plan provides a way for us and those we love.

Heavenly Father, when my world seems out of control, please help me love and trust You—even in the deserts of life.

Evening

I Don't Want To!

"And this shall come to pass if you diligently obey the voice of the LORD your God."
Zechariah 6:15 NKJV

God expects us to learn how to hear and follow through, no matter how we feel. It's the only way He can help us fulfill the plan He has for our lives. There will always be days when our feelings will pull us one way, while in our heart and spirit we know we shouldn't be listening to those feelings.

God, help me to walk in Your will every day.

MORNING

Overwhelmed by Life

"The waves of death swirled about me; the torrents of destruction overwhelmed me. . . . In my distress I called to the LORD. . . . From his temple he heard my voice; my cry came to his ears."
2 SAMUEL 22:5, 7 NIV

Next time you feel that you can't put one foot in front of the other, ask God to send you His strength and energy. He will help you to live out your purpose in this chaotic world.

Lord, thank You for strengthening me when the "dailyness" of life, and its various trials, threaten to overwhelm me.

EVENING

God Knows

You have searched me, LORD, and you know me.
PSALM 139:1 NIV

It's comforting to know God understands us. Sometimes our attitudes are right, but others misunderstand our intentions. If we ask God, He will help us communicate our true feelings to others in a way that they'll understand us better.

Dear Father, I'm so glad You understand me. Help me to think like You think.

DAY
40

MORNING

Ask for Directions

The wicked in his proud countenance does not seek God;
God is in none of his thoughts.
PSALM 10:4 NKJV

Somewhere along the way we got the idea that it is wrong to ask for help. But you can't live the Christian life like that. It's impossible. You can't possibly forge through life alone, managing to make wise decisions while you resist temptations and recover from failures. If you don't ask for help, you won't stand a chance.

Jesus, forgive me for my pride and for not asking You for directions.
Please show me the way to go and lead me in it.
Help me to hear Your leading and then to follow it. Amen.

EVENING

Soak It Up!

Oh, how I love your law! I meditate on it all day long.
PSALM 119:97 NIV

Soaking in God's Word every day will keep you balanced and ready to tackle whatever comes your way. You'll begin to bubble over with joy. You'll become a better person—a better friend, a better daughter, a better sister, a better mother, a better Christian—and you won't even get "pruney" in the process. So go ahead, girl. Soak it up!

God, thank You for Your Word. Help me to love it as much as You do. Amen.

Morning

Fishers of Men

"Come, follow Me," Jesus said,
"and I will send you out to fish for people."
Matthew 4:19 niv

Jesus came not only to save but to teach men and women how to have true servants' hearts. The substance of ministry is service. When the apostles agreed to follow Christ, they accepted the call on His terms, not theirs.

Lord, show me clearly where I can be of service within my local body of believers. Perhaps there's a small hand in Sunday school just waiting to be held.

Evening

A Giant Eraser

Let all that I am praise the Lord; may I never forget the good things he does for me. He forgives all my sins and heals all my diseases.
Psalm 103:2–3 nlt

Don't beat yourself up when you mess up. Just ask for forgiveness and then imagine God wiping away that bad stuff and giving you a chance to replace it with good. He will, you know. So why not stop right now and pray the following prayer:

Lord, what a relief to know that my mess-ups won't mess up my relationship with You. Thank You for that. Amen.

DAY
42

Morning

Melting Point

If anyone builds on that foundation with gold, silver, costly stones, wood, hay, or straw, each one's work will become obvious. . .because it will be revealed by fire.
1 Corinthians 3:12–13 HCSB

When we consider what we say, do, purchase, or pursue, we can use today's verse as our standard. Is our pursuit *ignitable*—temporary and unimportant—or is it *malleable*—something that can be reshaped and used as God directs?

O Lord God, You test me to transform me into the image of Your Son. Teach me to invest in what will last and not that which passes away.

Evening

Courage to Face the Hard Times

"Be strong and courageous. . .for it is the Lord *your God who goes with you. He will not leave you or forsake you."*
Deuteronomy 31:6 ESV

God doesn't want you to run from challenges; rather, He wants to face them with you. He inspires you to be strong because He will confront the hard time with you. No matter how rough it gets, there's nothing that can make Him leave you. He is with you through it all.

Dear Jesus, thank You for being such a faithful friend. Amen.

Morning

Discernment

And in His teaching He was saying: "Beware of the scribes. . . who devour widows' houses, and for appearance's sake offer long prayers; these will receive greater condemnation."
Mark 12:38, 40 NASB

All of us are responsible not only to read the Word of God with understanding but also to have discernment concerning the clergy who minister to us. Is their primary goal to make sure their flock is ultimately led to God's glory?

Am I like those in the crowd who simply "enjoyed listening" (Mark 12:37 NASB*) to Christ? Help me take time to know You, Lord.*

Evening

Sometimes Love Means Stop

The Lord disciplines the one he loves.
Hebrews 12:6 NIV

Because God loves you, there are times when He will tell you to stop. And sometimes the way He will get you—and me—to stop doing something that is hurtful for us is to discipline us. His discipline is always done in love because He cares for us and He doesn't want us to get hurt.

Lord, thank You that You discipline me. I am so very grateful that You don't allow me to do everything I want, especially when You know something is bad for me.

DAY 44

Morning

Take My Hand

I have no regrets. I couldn't be more sure of my ground—
the One I've trusted in can take care of what he's trusted me to do.
2 Timothy 1:11–12 msg

Are you sure today of the One you serve? When coming to grips with difficulties, do you turn to the Creator of the universe and ask for help? You should. He's available. Just reach out and take His hand. He'll be there.

Lord, teach me Your love. Let me feel Your embrace.
I choose to trust in You. Amen.

Evening

The Lord, Your Hero

Though I walk in the midst of trouble, you preserve my life.
You stretch out your hand against the anger of my foes;
with your right hand you save me.
Psalm 138:7 niv

God loves you and watches over you every moment of every day. His ears are always open to your prayers (1 Peter 3:12). Because of your relationship with Him, you can be confident that He will keep you safe. When you go to sleep at night, you can sleep peacefully.

Dear God, even though the world is a scary place,
I know I can count on You. Amen.

MORNING

How Do I Love Thee?

This is what real love is: It is not our love for God; it is God's love for us. He sent his Son to die in our place to take away our sins.
1 JOHN 4:10 NCV

The Bible tells us God does not *need* our love. He *is* love. God the Father, God the Son, and God the Spirit love each other in perfect eternal unity and joy. If God had done the logical thing, He would have wiped out us troublesome humans and created a new race, one that would worship Him without question. But He would rather die than do that.

Oh, Lord, open my eyes to Your magnificent generosity so I can worship with my whole heart, in a way that pleases You.

EVENING

Words of Comfort

This is my comfort in my affliction, for Your word has given me life.
PSALM 119:50 NKJV

Remember that our God wants only what is best for you, and then turn to Him. He is the Great Comforter. Reread today's verse from Psalm 119, and familiarize yourself with other scriptures about God's comfort. Be assured that He is *always* ready and willing to comfort you.

Dear heavenly Father, please give me comfort so that I can quit crying and get past my hurt. And please help me to comfort others when they feel like I do right now. Amen.

DAY
46

Morning

Light in the Darkness

I will lead blind Israel down a new path, guiding them along an unfamiliar way. I will brighten the darkness before them and smooth out the road ahead of them.
Isaiah 42:16 NLT

God will never leave us to find our way alone. Realize this truth and arm yourself with the knowledge that no matter what the situation, no matter what the trial, no matter how black the darkness, He is ever there, reaching out for us, helping us find our way.

Lord, be my light. Guard me in the darkness of these days. In Jesus' name, I pray. Amen.

Evening

If His Eye Is on the Sparrow. . .

"Look at the birds of the air, that they do not sow, nor reap nor gather into barns, and yet your heavenly Father feeds them. Are you not worth much more than they?"
Matthew 6:26 NASB

God: He understands. He sees what you're going through, and He's there to help you, strengthen you, and carry you through. He wants you to trust Him and know that He has everything under control. God will never abandon you, beloved.

God, I trust You, Lord. And I will keep trusting You. In Jesus' name I pray. Amen.

Morning

Hope

Why, my soul, are you downcast? Why so disturbed within me?
Put your hope in God, for I will yet praise him, my Savior and my God.
Psalm 42:5 NIV

Hope is like a little green shoot poking up through hard, cracked ground. When you're depressed, do what David and Jeremiah did—pour out your heart to God. Seek help from a trusted friend or godly counselor. Look for hope. It's all around you, and it's yours for the taking.

Father, even when I am depressed, You are still God.
Help me to find a ray of hope in the midst of dark circumstances. Amen.

Evening

Reading and Growing

Search the scriptures.
John 5:39 KJV

The Bible may have been written centuries ago, but its principles apply to your life today. No matter what situation you find yourself in, God's Word has the answer for how to handle it.

Dear God, put a love for the Bible in my heart.
Remind me to set aside some time each day to read the scriptures,
and most of all, help to me to obey what I read. Amen.

DAY
48

Morning

The Original "Me Generation"

And He called the twelve together, and gave them power and authority over all the demons and to heal diseases. And He sent them out to proclaim the kingdom of God and to perform healing.
Luke 9:1–2 nasb

These were the men Christ had trained, empowered, and prepared to bring the Gospel message first to the Jews and then the Gentiles. They had been with Christ on a daily basis, learning from His example how to reach out with compassion to those in need.

Lord, how grateful I am that Your Holy Spirit worked in the lives of these apostles, molding them into strong men of faith. Help me to become unselfish with my time that many more will hear the Gospel.

Evening

Joy in Problems

Consider it pure joy, my brothers and sisters, whenever you face trials of many kinds, because you know that the testing of your faith produces perseverance.
James 1:2–3 niv

Did you read that scripture right? Consider it *joy* when problems come into your life? *Really?* Yep, that's what God's Word says. This means that you "get" the fact that this world isn't perfect and problems will come—and that you trust in God to give you joy, in spite of the bad stuff!

Dear Jesus, help me to grow up knowing, loving, and trusting You—even during difficult times.

MORNING

Fear-Free

You will not fear the terror of night,
nor the arrow that flies by day.
PSALM 91:5 NIV

We serve an awesome and mighty God, One who longs to convince us He's mighty enough to save us, even when the darkness seeps in around us. So don't fear what you can't see. Or what you *can* see. Hand over that fear and watch God-ordained faith rise up in its place.

Father, sometimes I face the unseen things of my life with fear gripping my heart. I release that fear to You today. Thank You for replacing it with godly courage.

EVENING

Always, Always

It is God who arms me with
strength and keeps my way secure.
PSALM 18:32 NIV

Whenever you are feeling anxious, take a deep breath and talk to the heavenly Father. Tell Him exactly what you are feeling, and give all your worries to Him. He is listening and wants to hear from you—no matter what you have to say.

Heavenly Father, thank You for always watching over me and giving me strength when I feel weak. Help me to remember that when I'm feeling lost or scared. Amen.

DAY
50

Morning

Be a God Pleaser

Am I now trying to win the approval of human beings, or of God? Or am I trying to please people? If I were still trying to please people, I would not be a servant of Christ.
Galatians 1:10 NIV

Here's how the game works: We do our best to make others happy—at any expense. Our health, our finances, our time. Today, let's aim to be God pleasers. Let's do the things *He* calls us to—nothing more and nothing less.

Lord, You see my heart. You know what struggles I have in accomplishing these tasks. Redirect my thoughts, Father, to pleasing You rather than men.

Evening

Do Not Be Afraid

For God has not given us a spirit of fear, but of power and of love and of a sound mind.
2 Timothy 1:7 NKJV

God assures us in His Word that He knows the plans He has for us, and those plans are to bring us hope and a future. . .never to harm us (Jeremiah 29:11). Nothing can touch your life without first being filtered through the fingers of your heavenly Father.

God, sometimes I feel so afraid. Help me to remember that You have put a spirit of courage within me. Amen.

Morning

Pack Up!

The Lord had said to Abram, "Leave your native country, your relatives, and your father's family, and go to the land that I will show you. . . . I will bless you. . .and you will be a blessing to others."
Genesis 12:1–2 NLT

Are you facing a big change? God wants us to be willing to embrace change that He brings into our lives. Even unbidden change. You may feel as if you're out on a limb, but don't forget that God is the tree trunk. He's not going to let you fall.

Holy, loving Father, in every area of my life,
teach me to trust You more deeply. Amen.

Evening

The God Hug

Praise be to the God and Father of our Lord Jesus Christ, the Father of compassion and the God of all comfort, who comforts us in all our troubles, so that we can comfort those in any trouble.
2 Corinthians 1:3–4 NIV

No matter what's going on around us, we can always find that still, small voice in our spirit that says, *"I love you. I'll never leave you. I think you're special, and I want you to trust in Me and have peace."*

Dear Father, thank You for being my comforter.

DAY
52

Morning

When Fear Paralyzes

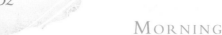

A young man was following Him, wearing nothing but a linen sheet over his naked body; and they seized him.
Mark 14:51 NASB

We know John Mark escaped the threatening situation. Yet Jesus Christ remained in the eye of the storm, well aware of the situation yet in perfect sync with the Father. When fear paralyzes, help is only a prayer away.

Lord, I believe in all that You are, both God and man.

Evening

Me, Strong?

It is God who arms me with strength and keeps my way secure.
Psalm 18:32 NIV

When you feel weak, don't allow feelings of insignificance to overwhelm you. God has given you *His* strength for each day. And His strength is perfect.

God, thank You for today and even for all the challenges that come my way. Thank You for giving me Your strength. Remind me in the hard times that Your strength is all I need. And help me to keep my focus on You. Amen.

MORNING

Talking to God

One of his disciples said to him, "Lord, teach us to pray, just as John taught his disciples." He said to them, "When you pray, say: 'Father, hallowed be your name, your kingdom come. Give us each day our daily bread.'"
LUKE 11:1–3 NIV

Luke 11 teaches us something beyond just an outline for prayer. The story shows clearly that if we ask God to teach us how to pray, He will. It's all part of the prayer—ask God to lead you; then speak to Him from the heart.

Dear God, teach me how to pray. Remind me that my words don't have to be profound. You're just looking for earnest thoughts from the heart.

EVENING

How Much Is Too Much?

For I am convinced that neither death nor life, neither angels nor demons, neither the present nor the future, nor any powers, neither height nor depth, nor anything else in all creation, will be able to separate us from the love of God that is in Christ Jesus our Lord.
ROMANS 8:38–39 NIV

God not only wants to forgive you but also hopes to be your best and closest friend.

Lord, forgive me for all the things I've done that make You sad, and help me to live closer to You each day so that I might know Your peace and joy! Amen.

DAY 54

Morning

Fix Your Eyes

So we fix our eyes not on what is seen, but on what is unseen, since what is seen is temporary, but what is unseen is eternal.
2 Corinthians 4:18 NIV

Spend your energy and resources on those things that will last: your relationships with your heavenly Father and with others. Love God. Love people. Then you won't fear being cut down like the majestic oak. You will live into eternity in the Lord's presence.

Dear Lord, help me keep an eternal focus and perspective in this life. Allow me to "see" what is unseen. Amen.

Evening

Not Looking My Best

"For the Lord does not see as man sees; for man looks at the outward appearance, but the Lord looks at the heart."
1 Samuel 16:7 NKJV

God knows the essence of who you are. And as you share your positive attitude and warm smile, the people around you will see the beauty of your heart, too! Heart beauty never has a bad hair day. It is *always* stylish.

God, thank You that even on a bad hair day my inner heart beauty comes shining through. Help me to always allow my heart to shine through in every situation. Amen.

Morning

Say What?

Don't fool yourself into thinking that you are a listener when you are anything but, letting the Word go in one ear and out the other. Act on what you hear!
James 1:22 MSG

So often we find ourselves tuning out the minister on Sunday morning or thinking about other things as we read our Bibles or sing hymns of praise. We pretend to hear, but we are really letting the Word of God go in one ear and out the other. Our minds must be disciplined to really listen to God's Word.

Dear Lord, please teach me to be attentive to Your Word. Help me to act on the things You teach me so that mine becomes a practical faith. Amen.

Evening

Needs and Wants

"That is why I tell you not to worry about everyday life— whether you have enough food or drink, or enough clothes to wear. Isn't life more than food, and your body more than clothing?"
Matthew 6:25 NLT

Be sure to thank God for all your blessings. When you have a thankful heart, you can look at all the blessings you've received with new eyes.

Lord, help me to remember all the wonderful blessings You've given me and let me focus on the important things in life, not material things. Amen.

DAY
56

MORNING

Martha and Mary

"Lord, do You not care that my sister has left me to do all the serving alone? Then tell her to help me."
LUKE 10:40 NASB

Isn't this just how we feel when the men in our household excuse themselves from the table as soon as the first dirty dish appears? Martha, ever the perfect hostess, was left to do all the work.

Have you taken time to get to know your Lord? Perhaps your life, like Martha's, is missing the best part.

Lord, I pray for peace today from my busy schedule so I may learn at Your knee.

EVENING

In His Care

And my God will supply all your needs according to His riches in glory in Christ Jesus.
PHILIPPIANS 4:19 NASB

Because God is our God of unconditional love, He will give us some "wants," too. He is a loving Father who joys in showering blessings on His children.

Trust that He knows what your needs are versus your wants! He owns it all—we only look after it for the time He places it in our care.

Dear heavenly Father, thank You for giving me all that I need. Help me to trust that You will take care of me.

MORNING

Humble Service Is Pure Religion

Pure religion and undefiled before God and the Father is this, to visit the fatherless and widows in their affliction, and to keep himself unspotted from the world.
JAMES 1:27 KJV

How do you want to be remembered? The world remembers wealth, fame, and accomplishments, but God recognizes the small, daily kindnesses shown to others. Keep that in mind as you go through the day.

Dear Father, please remind me that greatness in Your eyes comes in humility and lowliness, in caring for those who have afflictions. Thank You for the many opportunities You give me to serve.

EVENING

The Cowardly Lion

"Be strong and of good courage, do not fear nor be afraid of them; for the LORD your God, He is the One who goes with you. He will not leave you nor forsake you."
DEUTERONOMY 31:6 NKJV

Today, if you're struggling to be courageous, ask God to give you His courage. Then look your fear in the eye and say, "You don't scare me anymore!" Watch those fears. . .disappear!

God, thank You for giving me the courage I need to face the hard things! Amen.

DAY 58

Morning

Red High Heels

You should clothe yourselves instead with the beauty that comes from within, the unfading beauty of a gentle and quiet spirit, which is so precious to God.
1 Peter 3:4 NLT

Shoes scuff, necklaces break, and fabric fades, but true beauty starts from within. When we allow God to dress our spirits in robes of love, joy, peace, patience, kindness, goodness, faithfulness, gentleness, and self-control, our inner beauty will far outshine anything we put on our physical bodies.

Dear Father, I want to be a woman whose inner beauty far surpasses my outer beauty, so that when people see me they are pointed to You and rejoice in Your creation.

Evening

When You Lose a Friend

The Lord is close to the brokenhearted
and saves those who are crushed in spirit.
Psalm 34:18 NIV

No matter how you feel, if you are mad, sad, or frustrated, God cares. When you lose someone special to you, God wants to comfort you. He is always there. He wants to heal your broken heart. Tell Him how you feel, and listen for His voice. He loves you.

Lord Jesus, when my heart is broken, help me to trust that You will heal me and help me to keep my heart open so that I can keep loving others.

MORNING

Where Do You Take Refuge?

When I am afraid, I will put my trust in You. In God, whose word I praise, in God I have put my trust; I shall not be afraid. What can mere man do to me?
PSALM 56:3–4 NASB

Where do you go for refuge? I run to the arms of my loving Father, just as David did in his own crisis. And He always comes through.

O Lord, You alone are my refuge and strength.
Help me to come to You first in a crisis.

EVENING

A Special Kind of Hope

Rejoice in our confident hope.
Be patient in trouble, and keep on praying.
ROMANS 12:12 NLT

One ingredient mentioned in these verses is hope. Not just any hope, but *confident* hope. *Confident* hope is a sure thing. . .like the hope of God's love and a future home in heaven. These things are guaranteed if we have chosen to follow Jesus. We can have this kind of hope all the time. It's a special gift—a gift that God gives to us as a promise.

Dear Lord, I will rejoice in the hope You have given me. Amen.

DAY 60

Morning

Microwave Faith?

And so after waiting patiently,
Abraham received what was promised.
HEBREWS 6:15 NIV

How many times have you given up on the promises of God because circumstances told you something different? It's not too late. Pick up your faith. Determine to see those promises come to pass.

Heavenly Father, I ask You to forgive me for doubting You. I believe Your Word. I praise You and glorify You in advance for the promises You are bringing into my life.

Evening

Watch Your Words

Let everything you say be good and helpful, so that your
words will be an encouragement to those who hear them.
EPHESIANS 4:29 NLT

God wants us to be an encouragement to the people in our lives. He wants us to be helpful and to say things that make Him smile. He doesn't want us to use bad words or gossip about others, either. In James 1:26, the Bible tells us that if we claim to be Christians but gossip, our faith probably doesn't mean much to us.

Dear God, help me to honor You with my words. Amen.

MORNING

It's All Good

And we know that all things work together for good to them that love God, to them who are the called according to his purpose.
ROMANS 8:28 KJV

God can and does use all things in our lives for His good purpose. Remember Joseph in the cistern, Daniel in the lions' den, and Jesus on the cross? The Lord demonstrated His resurrection power in each of those cases. He does so in our lives as well. He brings forth beauty from ashes.

Dear Lord, thank You that You work all things together for Your good purpose. May I trust You to fulfill Your purpose in my life. Amen.

EVENING

How Hungry Are You?

For he satisfies the thirsty and fills the hungry with good things.
PSALM 107:9 NIV

If you're less than hungry for more of God, ask Him to increase your spiritual hunger. So go ahead—dig into God's Word today.

Thank You, God, for giving me physical food to feed my body. Please increase my spiritual hunger so that I may grow closer to You. Amen.

DAY
62

Morning

Calmed by His Love

"The Lord your God is in your midst, a mighty one who will save; he will rejoice over you with gladness; he will quiet you by his love; he will exult over you with loud singing."
Zephaniah 3:17 ESV

God's love sent His Son to die for you, that you might receive everything you need pertaining to life and godliness. His love enables you to keep on going even when you're ready to give up.

Father, I thank You for the gift of Your love. It calms me, it soothes me, it gives me peace in the middle of the storm. Please fill me with Your love and peace today.

Evening

Please Forgive Me

I acknowledged my sin to You, and my iniquity I have not hidden.
I said, "I will confess my transgressions to the Lord,"
and You forgave the iniquity of my sin.
Psalm 32:5 NKJV

When you know you've done wrong, remember that God knows *all* you do and *nothing* is hidden from Him. But He is a God of mercy and forgiveness. All you have to do is ask!

Dear God, please forgive me for my sin. I thank You for being a forgiving God. Please give me strength and wisdom to make the best decisions in the future. Amen.

MORNING

When Everyone in Heaven Rejoices

"I tell you, there is joy in the presence of the angels of God over one sinner who repents."
LUKE 15:10 NASB

Jesus compared a woman's deep joy at finding her lost coin to the celebration that goes on in heaven when a sinner repents and "Son-beams" of peace finally flood into the soul. It's the feeling of "wholeness" a person hungers for all her life.

Lord, I am grateful that Your Word has penetrated the core of my own heart. Hallelujah!

EVENING

I Think I Can; I Think I Can!

"Fear not, for I am with you; be not dismayed, for I am your God; I will strengthen you, yes, I will help you, I will uphold you with My righteous right hand."
ISAIAH 41:10 NKJV

God promises to be there with you through all those hard times and to carry your fears. He will give you the strength you need to live out His call in your life, and He'll never ask you to do anything that He won't equip you to do.

Dear God, please give me the strength today to do the things You ask me to do. Amen.

DAY
64

MORNING

Commitment Challenges

Remember me for this, my God, and do not blot out what I have so faithfully done for the house of my God and its services.
NEHEMIAH 13:14 TNIV

Nehemiah fought enemies, settled internal squabbles and—and—*and!* His days never seemed long enough. He grew discouraged when trusted fellow workers in God's house placed their priorities elsewhere. Between crises, Nehemiah took a deep breath and prayed the above prayer.

Like you, Nehemiah may not have seen his reward as soon as he wanted. But now he is enjoying it forever.

So will you.

Lord Jesus, when I feel tired and unappreciated as I serve others, let Your applause be enough for me.

EVENING

The Real Hope

My soul, wait only upon God and silently submit to Him; for my hope and expectation are from Him.
PSALM 62:5 AMP

The only real hope comes from Jesus Christ. He is always right there—He doesn't move away or leave us on our own. That's hope we can count on!

He will *be* our true hope and will *give* us true hope—especially in those times that seem to be hopeless.

Dear Lord Jesus, thank You for being my true hope and for giving me true hope. In Your name, amen.

Morning

Think Big

"For as the sky soars high above earth, so the way I work surpasses the way you work, and the way I think is beyond the way you think."
ISAIAH 55:9 MSG

We should dream big and ask God for direction in life. We humans are impatient and want what we want right now. But our Father in heaven knows better. He has created a world that unfolds according to His timetable.

*Dear Lord, You know my heart's desire.
Help me to wait upon Your answer for my life. Amen.*

Evening

The Right Thing—Every Time

Because you obey the LORD your God by keeping all his commands that I am giving you today and doing what is right in his eyes.
DEUTERONOMY 13:18 NIV

Ever had one of those days? . . . Nothing goes right, you're running late on the way to work. You spill coffee all over your outfit. When these days happen, take a breath and remember that God understands.

*God, forgive me, Lord, for all the times
I've failed to listen to Your voice. Amen.*

DAY
66

Morning

Our Prayer Requests

In the morning, Lord, you hear my voice; in the morning I lay my requests before you and wait expectantly.
Psalm 5:3 NIV

On Sunday evenings I ask my husband and children for any particular things they'd like me to pray about for the coming week. Such concerns as tests, projects, or schoolwork that are due, and once in a while concerns of class bullies or teachers will be voiced.

Are you laying your own requests before the Lord?

Lord, I wander around like those who have no hope, forgetting to ask You for wise solutions to my dilemmas. Help me remember to come to You before I start my day.

Evening

Give Him Your Dreams

Humble yourselves before the Lord, and he will lift you up.
James 4:10 NIV

Remember that God always knows best. Also remember that He will never ask you to give up something without giving something in return that is His best plan. His plan may not always be easy, but it will be right, and you will be happy that you followed Him. You can trust His plan.

Lord, sometimes it's hard for me to give up what I want for what You want. Help me to trust You and not to demand my own way. Amen.

Morning

Financial Strain

"No one can serve two masters. Either you will hate the one and love the other, or you will be devoted to the one and despise the other. You cannot serve both God and money."
MATTHEW 6:24 NIV

As you feel yourself start to worry about money, stop and change your focus from wealth to God. Thank Him for what He has provided for you and then humbly ask Him to give you wisdom about your financial situation.

Dear God, help me not to worry but to trust that You will provide for me. Help me to be devoted to You only. Amen.

Evening

You're Gonna Live Forever!

And this is the testimony: God has given us eternal life, and this life is in his Son.
1 JOHN 5:11 NIV

When God sent Jesus to die on the cross, Jesus paid the price for Adam's sins and everyone who came after him—including you. Through Jesus Christ you can have a relationship with the Creator of the universe and cheat death at the same time!

Dear God, thank You for making a way for me to escape death and live a life of joy and peace forever with You. Amen.

DAY
68

Morning

A Discerning Woman

Wisdom reposes in the heart of the discerning
and even among fools she lets herself be known.
Proverbs 14:33 niv

Today's proverb says that "wisdom reposes in the heart of the discerning." Remember that whenever you cross paths with someone who is hurting. Use discernment to love that person well.

Lord, everyone has a cross to bear. But because You bore
Calvary's cross for me, I have the hope of eternal life.

Evening

God's Workmanship

For we are His workmanship, created in Christ Jesus for good works,
which God prepared beforehand so that we would walk in them.
Ephesians 2:10 nasb

God sees you as His workmanship and craftsmanship. He loves you beyond measure, precious one. Trust Him. He knows what He's doing. (See Proverbs 3:5; Ephesians 4:20–24; Colossians 2:13–14; 1 Peter 3:3–4.)

God, I know that I'm beautiful in Your eyes. Thank You for loving me,
covering me with Your fingerprints, and having a plan for me.
I love You. Thank You so much. In Jesus' name I pray. Amen.

MORNING

Release the Music Within

Those who are wise will find a time
and a way to do what is right.
ECCLESIASTES 8:5 NLT

Whether we are eight or eighty, it is never too late to surrender our hopes and dreams to God. A wise woman trusts that God will help her find the time and manner in which to use her talents for His glory as she seeks His direction.

Let the music begin.

Dear Lord, my music is fading against the constant beat of a busy pace. I surrender my gifts to You and pray for the time and manner in which I can use those gifts to touch my world. Amen.

EVENING

The Great Comforter

God is our merciful Father and the source of all comfort.
He comforts us in all our troubles so that we can comfort others.
2 CORINTHIANS 1:3–4 NLT

God loves you with an everlasting love. When you need to be comforted, tell God. He is always there, and it brings Him great pleasure when you choose Him as your comforter.

God, there are some areas of my life where I am hurting. Be my comforter, I pray. Amen.

DAY
70

MORNING

God's Foolishness Is Human Wisdom

For the foolishness of God is wiser than human wisdom,
and the weakness of God is stronger than human strength.
1 CORINTHIANS 1:25 NIV

This is faith in God. Sometimes, He'll lead us to act contrary to common sense. Did it "make sense" to have Jesus Christ die for our sins? How could a man, hanging on a cross outside Jerusalem, take away our sins? It's foolishness. Impossible!

Believing God brings the deep peace that comes with that decision.

Lord, I thank You that You go before me in every choice, even the confusing ones!
I can move forward with confidence, knowing You are with me.

EVENING

What Do I Have to Look Forward To?

"For my Father's will is that everyone who looks to the Son and believes
in him shall have eternal life, and I will raise them up at the last day."
JOHN 6:40 NIV

No matter where you are today—excited about the future or not—remember that the very best is yet to come. An eternity without pain or sorrow or sadness.

Now that's something to look forward to.

God, sometimes I don't feel I have much to look forward to,
but help me remember that the best is yet to come.
Please help me to share that with someone else today. Amen.

MORNING

Reach Out

But people who aren't spiritual can't receive these truths from God's Spirit. It all sounds foolish to them and they can't understand it, for only those who are spiritual can understand what the Spirit means.
1 CORINTHIANS 2:14 NLT

God likely has placed unbelievers in your life that He wants you to reach out to. Share your faith with them in words and actions they can understand. Pray the Lord opens their hearts to receive Jesus as Lord and Savior.

Dear Lord, help me not to judge those who don't know You. Instead, may I pray that You intercede to show them the way. Amen.

EVENING

All Prayed Out

Then Jesus told his disciples a parable to show them that they should always pray and not give up.
LUKE 18:1 NIV

No matter what you are praying about, don't give up! Keep talking to the heavenly Father. The process of persistent prayer will change your heart to be more like His. And at times when you feel all prayed out, remember that God is *always* listening and working in your life.

God, help me not to lose heart but to remember Your love and faithfulness. Amen.

DAY
72

Morning

Weary Days

O my God, my soul is cast down within me: therefore will I remember thee from the land of Jordan, and of the Hermonites, from the hill Mizar.
Psalm 42:6 KJV

Our willingness to speak with God at the day's beginning shows our dependence on Him. We can't make it alone. It is a comforting truth that God never intended for us to trek through the hours unaccompanied. He promises to be with us. He also promises His guidance and direction as we meet people and receive opportunities to serve Him.

Lord, refresh my spirit and give me joy for today's activities. Amen.

Evening

A Giant Treasure Box

My God will use his wonderful riches in Christ Jesus to give you everything you need.
Philippians 4:19 NCV

God doesn't give us what we want; He gives us what we need. So pray and let Him know the desires of your heart. Then watch His treasure box open as new gifts—perfect for you—are placed into your hands.

God, I know that I don't always get what I want. I remember that sometimes I would ask my parents for things and wouldn't get them. But You know what I really need. Thank You for providing for me! Amen.

MORNING

The Gift of Manna

They asked, and He brought quail,
and satisfied them with the bread of heaven.
PSALM 105:40 NASB

Another life-giving bread is symbolically offered to us under the new covenant. Jesus said, "I am the living bread that came down out of heaven; if anyone eats of this bread, he will live forever; and the bread also which I will give for the life of the world is My flesh" (John 6:51 NASB).

Lord, I long to live forever in Your glorious presence.

EVENING

Lesson from the Sea

He gave the sea its boundary so the
waters would not overstep his command.
PROVERBS 8:29 NIV

Even the ocean has boundaries. When God made the world, He put a limit on those great salty waters. Landlubbers rest easy knowing that no matter how fiercely the waves may surge inland, they can only go so far. If the sea could refuse to obey the rules, imagine the destruction it would cause!

Lord, help me to remember that I need to set boundaries for myself.
Give me wisdom and discernment about how to set them up.

DAY
74

MORNING

Restoration

He maketh me to lie down in green pastures:
he leadeth me beside the still waters. He restoreth my soul.
PSALM 23:2–3 KJV

God watches over us day and night, no matter where we are. He tends our wounds, guards us, and builds us back up for the challenges of life. When we are lost, we need only listen for the voice of our Shepherd.

Lord, my Shepherd, I shall not want. Teach me to lie still in Your green pastures and drink of Your quiet waters. Please restore my soul.

EVENING

Who Could Know You Better?

"And the very hairs on your head are all numbered. So don't be afraid; you are more valuable to God than a whole flock of sparrows."
LUKE 12:7 NLT

God knows each part of you. He is proud of His special creation—the perfect picture of you. He also knows your thoughts and dreams. . .the desires of your heart. God's knowing goes far deeper than we can even understand. And because His knowing is so deep, His love is deep, too. And that's the best blessing of all!

Heavenly Father, thank You for knowing me and loving me—no matter what. Amen.

MORNING

Mutual Delight Society

He brought me forth also into a large place:
he delivered me, because he delighted in me.
2 SAMUEL 22:20 KJV

The woman who delights in God has God delighting in her, too. His plans for her future are beautiful because she has experienced His salvation. No good thing will He deny her (though her definition of a good thing and His may differ at times).

Do you delight in God? Then share the news. Help others join this mutual delight society today.

Thank You, Lord, for inviting me to share Your delights. Amen.

EVENING

Mirror, Mirror

Don't be concerned about the outward beauty. . . .You should clothe yourselves instead with the beauty that comes from within. . .which is so precious to God.
1 PETER 3:3–4 NLT

All those other things that you might use to make yourself more outwardly beautiful cost money, time, and effort. But the gift of inner beauty that comes from knowing God and letting Him shine through you is always free.

Dear God, please help me see myself the way You see me.
Help me not to be so critical of my outward appearance and
to care more about reflecting You from the inside out. Amen.

DAY 76

MORNING

Vocalizing a Prayer

"And when you are praying, do not use meaningless repetition as the Gentiles do, for they suppose that they will be heard for their many words."
MATTHEW 6:7 NASB

As we come before the Lord, we first need to honor Him as Creator, Master, Savior, and Lord. Reflect on who He is and praise Him. And because we're human, we need to confess and repent of our daily sins. Following this we should be in a mode of thanksgiving.

Lord, Your Word says that my prayers rise up to heaven like incense from the earth. Remind me daily to send a sweet savor Your way!

EVENING

More Than Cherubs

"I give them eternal life, and they will never perish, and no one will snatch them out of my hand."
JOHN 10:28 ESV

As a Christian, you have so much to look forward to. No one really knows for sure what heaven will hold, but you can rest assured that it will be beyond your wildest dreams. There will be infinite joy, overwhelming beauty, and—best of all—you will get to see Jesus face-to-face.

God, when I get discouraged or anxious, help me to remember that this isn't my true home.

Morning

Answered Prayer

Delight yourself in the LORD; and He
will give you the desires of your heart.
PSALM 37:4 NASB

So what pleases God? He loves it when we witness for Him, live right, and instruct others in His Word. If those are things that we also truly desire, won't He grant us the "desires of our heart" and let us see people brought into the kingdom? Won't we have a life rich in spiritual growth?

Lord, please help me see where my desires are not in line with Your will—
so that the things that I pursue are only and always according to Your own desires.

Evening

Don't Give Up!

God began doing a good work in you, and I am sure he will
continue it until it is finished when Jesus Christ comes again.
PHILIPPIANS 1:6 NCV

We're not very good at carrying through sometimes, are we! Aren't you glad that God is? He doesn't start something and not finish it. That should give you hope! He began a good work in you, and He's going to complete it!

Lord, sometimes I start things but don't finish them. They seem too hard!
I give up hope. Thank You, God, for never giving up on me!
I want to learn from Your example! Amen.

DAY
78

Morning

Protecting Angels

For he will command his angels concerning
you to guard you in all your ways.
Psalm 91:11 NIV

Take great comfort in knowing that God loves you so much that you are being guarded and protected by an elite group of heavenly host.

Dear Lord, no matter where I go, in my heart I always know that Your angels are with me night and day, keeping me safe in every way. Amen.

Evening

A Fresh Start

He has removed our sins as far from
us as the east is from the west.
Psalm 103:12 NLT

God wipes the record clean. He forgives us. The verse above says He removes our sins as far as the east is from the west. And since the east and west never meet each other, that's a pretty long way.

Dear Father, I'm sorry for my mistakes.
Thank You for giving me a fresh start.

MORNING

Music in the Morning

For You, O LORD, have made me glad by what You have done,
I will sing for joy at the works of Your hands.
PSALM 92:4 NASB

This particular psalm was actually written for a Sabbath celebration. They sing, dance, and rejoice in finding their Savior. It's the kind of merriment God designed for us to enjoy with Him. And it's probably the closest reenactment of heavenly worship you'll find on this earth.

Lord, thank You for music and the way it uplifts my spirits.
No matter what time of day or season, I rejoice in worshipping You.

EVENING

A Joyful Heart

A cheerful heart is good medicine,
but a broken spirit saps a person's strength.
PROVERBS 17:22 NLT

Whatever today brings, try to keep an attitude of joy. It may change the results, or it may not. But either way, resting in God and trusting that He will work everything out for His good is the best way to go.

Dear Jesus, I want to be a person with a joyful heart.
Please help me to trust that You are working good in my life,
whether I can see the results right now or not. Amen.

DAY 80

Morning

Powerful One

He who forms the mountains, who creates the wind, and who reveals his thoughts to mankind, who turns dawn to darkness, and treads on the heights of the earth—the Lord God Almighty is his name.
Amos 4:13 NIV

Problems that seem insurmountable to us are simply a breath to Him. Let's not be anxious today—God holds each one of us in the palm of His hand.

Lord God, You are my Provider. Thank You for holding such power—and for choosing me to be Your child. Please give me a greater understanding of who You are, helping me to remember that You, the Lord God Almighty, love me.

Evening

Band-Aid Moments

I will speak with the voice of thanks, and tell of all Your great works.
Psalm 26:7 NLV

The next time you encounter a bad situation, try to view it from God's perspective. Your attitude might change from "Life isn't fair!" to "Thank You, God! That was a close one!"

God, help me to see the big picture in my Band-Aid moments. I'm glad You're always there to protect me. Amen.

Morning

Simply Silly

A cheerful disposition is good for your health.
Proverbs 17:22 MSG

Is your cup of joy full? Have you laughed today? Not a small smile, but laughter. Maybe it's time we looked for something to laugh about and tasted joy. God suggested it.

Lord, help me find joy this day.
Let me laugh and give praises to the King. Amen.

Evening

He Hears Me

When the righteous cry for help, the Lord hears
and delivers them out of all their troubles.
Psalm 34:17 ESV

Do you ever wonder if God hears your prayers for help when everything seems to be going wrong? . . . When you feel sick or are depressed? . . . Or when you don't get everything you ask for? . . . Sometimes we forget all that God has done for us or how many prayers He's answered. Thank God for answered prayers!

Dear God, please help me to remember
that You always hear my prayers. Amen.

DAY
82

Morning

Finding the Messiah

He found first his own brother Simon and said to him,
"We have found the Messiah" (which translated means Christ).
John 1:41 NASB

How blessed for Andrew that his brother responded and they shared the love of the Lord together. In many families this never happens. Perhaps in reading this you understand what it means to be ridiculed because of your faith in Christ.

Lord, I pray for strength to share
Your love with unbelieving family members.

Evening

Join the Clutter-Free Club

In his pride the wicked man does not seek him;
in all his thoughts there is no room for God.
Psalm 10:4 NIV

God is the best organizer, the best planner, and the best time manager. (He did create the whole world in less than a week!) The Bible says to seek Him first. When you do, all the clutter just seems to fall away, and God supernaturally organizes your day.

God, please help me declutter my life. Thank You! Amen.

MORNING

Action-Figure Easter

We will not hide these truths from our children;
we will tell the next generation about the glorious deeds of the LORD.
PSALM 78:4 NLT

Michelle treasured her children's delight each Easter morning when they sprang from their beds to find the grave handkerchief discarded and Jesus miraculously sitting atop the shoe-box tomb, His little plastic arms raised triumphantly in the air.

Risen Savior, help us use every opportunity to instill in our children the marvelous truths of our faith, so that Your love may be as a precious heirloom to future generations. Amen.

EVENING

The Lord Is Faithful

But the Lord is faithful, and He will strengthen
and protect you from the evil one.
2 THESSALONIANS 3:3 NASB

You're given truth, righteousness, the Gospel of peace, faith, salvation, and the magnificent Word of God—all of these to wield unceasingly, in faith that God has provided and will protect you.

Father, thank You for keeping me safe. Thank You for protection and peace. Thank You for Your Word, salvation, truth, and righteousness. I will trust You, Lord. With all my heart. In Jesus' name I pray. Amen.

DAY
84

Morning

Anxious Anticipations

I am not saying this because I am in need,
for I have learned to be content whatever the circumstances.
Philippians 4:11 NIV

Humans have a tendency to complain about the problems and irritations of life. It's much less natural to appreciate the good things we have—until they're gone. While it's fine to look forward to the future, let's remember to reflect on all of *today's* blessings—the large and the small—and appreciate all that we do have.

Thank You, Lord, for the beauty of today. Please remind me when I become preoccupied with the future and forget to enjoy the present.

Evening

With Grace

Now this is the confidence that we have in Him,
that if we ask anything according to His will, He hears us.
1 John 5:14 NKJV

God either meets that need by giving you exactly what you asked for, or He meets it with *no* or sometimes a *maybe*. But even in the *no* and the *maybe* there is still action. He decides what's the very best for us, and He is going to provide that even if it means saying *no*.

Dear God, please help me to accept the no's and the not-yets with grace.

MORNING

The Passover Lamb

"For the LORD will pass through to smite the Egyptians; and when He sees the blood on the lintel and on the two doorposts, the LORD will pass over the door and will not allow the destroyer to come to your houses to smite you."
EXODUS 12:23 NASB

We can celebrate the Passover with joy and thanksgiving, knowing for certain that the long-awaited Messiah has come and will come again!

Lord Jesus Christ, I thank You for being my promised Messiah and Passover Lamb. I thank You for Your sacrifice so that my sins could be forgiven.

EVENING

God Provides

"Look at the birds of the air; they do not sow or reap or store away in barns, and yet your heavenly Father feeds them. Are you not much more valuable than they?"
MATTHEW 6:26 NIV

True happiness doesn't come from our belongings but from a genuine relationship with God. Start today by thanking Him for the way He provides all that you need. Then challenge yourself to say a prayer of thanksgiving whenever you begin to feel even the slightest tinge of jealousy.

Thank You, Lord, for Your many blessings. Amen.

DAY
86

Morning

Refreshing Gift

For we have great joy and consolation in your love,
because the hearts of the saints have been refreshed by you, brother.
PHILEMON 1:7 NKJV

God brings people into our path who need our encouragement. We must consider those around us. Smile and thank the waitress, the cashier, the people who help in small ways. Cheering others can have the effect of an energizing drink of water so that they will be able to finish the race with a smile.

Jesus, thank You for being an example of how to encourage and refresh others. Help me to see their need and to be willing to reach out. Amen.

Evening

A Special Message

The people read it and were glad for its encouraging message.
ACTS 15:31 NIV

When you're through spending time in God's Word, you'll have time to reflect and write in a journal or diary. And the best part? . . . You'll find yourself growing closer to the heavenly Father *every day*!

God, please help me to stay faithful, spending time in Your Word every day. Thank You! Amen.

MORNING

Give It All

Jesus looked him hard in the eye—and loved him! He said, "There's one thing left: Go sell whatever you own and give it to the poor. All your wealth will then be heavenly wealth. And come follow me."
MARK 10:21 MSG

What has Christ asked *you* to let go of? What are you holding tightly to? Most of us don't have great wealth (we might wish for that kind of "problem"), but are we willing to give up what we *do* have to serve Him?

Lord, show me what I need to relinquish to You. Help me to abandon everything to freely and joyfully serve You.

EVENING

In the Garden

You will always harvest what you plant. . . . Those who live to please the Spirit will harvest everlasting life from the Spirit.
GALATIANS 6:7–8 NLT

You can learn a lot by hanging out in a garden. But if you're not a big fan of digging in the dirt, just soak in all the beautiful flowers and plants that God created. View them as reminders that God wants you to do the right thing and grow into a woman who harvests "love, joy, peace, patience, kindness, goodness, faithfulness, gentleness, and self-control" (Galatians 5:22–23 NLT).

God, show my how to harvest the fruit of the spirit.

MORNING

What Is Written on Your Heart?

These commandments that I give you today are to be on your hearts. . . .
Write them on the doorframes of your houses and on your gates.
DEUTERONOMY 6:6, 9 NIV

What are some practical ways you can remind yourself, each day, of the truth of God's Word? Copy verses on index cards to carry with you, or better yet, commit them to memory. Whatever you do, always be looking for fresh ways to remember the truth that God has written on your heart.

Father, thank You for writing Your truth upon my heart.
Help me to look for tangible reminders of Your truth. Amen.

....

EVENING

A Man of His Word

If we are faithless, he remains faithful,
for he cannot disown himself.
2 TIMOTHY 2:13 NIV

If God says He will always be with you. . .He will. If He says He will protect you from your enemies. . .He will. If He says He will provide for your needs. . .He will. God is a man of His word. What He says He will do. . .He does!

Dear God, thank You for being a man of
Your word who keeps all of His promises. Amen.

MORNING

Look Around

Come and see the works of God;
He is awesome in His doing toward the sons of men.
PSALM 66:5 NKJV

God uplifts us through His Word. Just by reading the Bible, we're reminded of the grace and love God has for us. Then there's His creation. Watching a bird fly, seeing a squirrel scramble up a tree, and observing a beautiful flower or a wonderful sunrise are just a few ways God reminds us of His power. Encouragement can also be found by remembering what God has done for us.

Dear God, I thank You for all the ways You encourage me. May I not overlook Your blessings because they didn't come in the form I expected.

EVENING

God Won't Break His Promises

Let us hold unswervingly to the hope we profess,
for he who promised is faithful.
HEBREWS 10:23 NIV

It's easy to doubt God in our humanness. We are imperfect, so it's hard to understand how He can be perfect and all-knowing, all-powerful, all-present, and love us so much that He sacrificed His own Son to die for us. Other people may break their promises, but God won't. He doesn't lie.

God, I sometimes find myself doubting the truth of Your Word. Please forgive me and help me to remember Your promises. I love You, Lord. Amen.

DAY
90

Morning

Jesus Prepares His Disciples

And He took the twelve aside and said to them, "Behold we are going up to Jerusalem, and all things which are written through the prophets about the Son of Man will be accomplished."
LUKE 18:31 NASB

Jesus had traveled with the Twelve and lived out a sinless life before them. Now His time on earth drew to its inevitable close. He needed to help them accept His death, understand the reason for it, and strengthen them for all this would mean once they could no longer be with Him face-to-face.

I know the days ahead may be difficult. Help me realize, like the disciples, that You are always with me, to the end.

Evening

Forgiven: No More Bad Labels

If we confess our sins, he is faithful and just and will forgive us our sins and purify us from all unrighteousness.
1 JOHN 1:9 NIV

Remember that if you did something wrong today, it doesn't have to be your label tomorrow, because God forgives you and He will still use you.

Lord, I am so grateful You never say that because I sin, You won't forgive me. You always give me another chance. And You will always give me things to do for You. Amen.

MORNING

Thinking of Others

Not looking to your own interests but
each of you to the interests of the others.
PHILIPPIANS 2:4 NIV

When you start to look out for "number one," remember that your God is looking out for you. You are His precious daughter. As you allow Him to take care of you, it will free up space in your heart and allow you to look to the needs of others.

Father, You have made me to be a part of something much larger than myself. Focus my attention on those around me and not only on my own needs. Amen.

EVENING

Where Is God?

"I will never fail you. I will never abandon you."
HEBREWS 13:5 NLT

When we know God in a personal way, He will speak softly to our hearts, telling us He is there. He will always be there to answer questions and hear our cries twenty-four hours a day.

He will *never* leave you. Learn to listen for His voice.

Dear Father, I know You are with me, and I want to hear You speak to me. Help me turn to You when I am in trouble. Thank You for being by my side every minute of every day. Amen.

DAY
92

Morning

Wimps for Jesus?

Wherefore lift up the hands which hang down, and the feeble knees; and make straight paths for your feet, lest that which is lame be turned out of the way; but let it rather be healed.
HEBREWS 12:12–13 KJV

God presents better solutions for our problems. He disciplines us for the same reason a mother corrects her children: out of love. How can we think God wants any less for us?

Lord Jesus, please help me to obey You, trusting that You know what You're doing in my life.

Evening

Just Trust!

GOD, treat us kindly. You're our only hope. First thing in the morning, be there for us! When things go bad, help us out!
ISAIAH 33:2 MSG

Whenever you feel discouraged or hopeless, take the time to tell your heavenly Father and ask Him to fill you with hope. God loves His children and wants the absolute best for you. He wants to bless you with His peace and joy. Just ask, and He will provide.

Dear God, I trust that You are in control and will give me peace and joy in any situation. Amen.

MORNING

Knowing God's Precepts

Teach me Your statutes. Make me understand the way of Your precepts, so I will meditate on Your wonders.
PSALM 119:26–27 NASB

Confession of sin is the beginning of true hope. For when we acknowledge that we've failed, God can use our broken and contrite heart, through the Holy Spirit, to mold us anew.

Understand and walk in the way of the precepts by meditating on God's Word. If you're not participating in an in-depth Bible study, consider finding or starting one.

Lord, teach me Your ways, that I might live out our precepts before my family and loved ones.

EVENING

Got the Giggles?

May the God of hope fill you with all joy and peace as you trust in him, so that you may overflow with hope by the power of the Holy Spirit.
ROMANS 15:13 NIV

Don't worry about the tough stuff you're going through. Just ask God to give you His joy so that you can giggle your way through the tough times. He will do it! And when He does. . .watch out!

Lord, I don't always feel joyful. Sometimes I get sad. But now I know that I can ask for Your joy and You will put a smile on my face! I'm so glad! Amen.

DAY
94

MORNING

Wish List

But they cried the more, saying, Have mercy on us, O Lord,
thou Son of David. And Jesus stood still, and called them,
and said, What will ye that I shall do unto you?
MATTHEW 20:31–32 KJV

God doesn't *need* us to tell Him our desires. He already knows them. But He delights in going above and beyond what we can ask for. Even if He doesn't give us what we want, it's because He has something better in store.

Heavenly Father, I thank You that You care about the smallest details of my life. Teach me the joy of specific prayer.

EVENING

God Is Always with Me

"And the LORD, He is the One who goes before you. He will be with you,
He will not leave you nor forsake you; do not fear nor be dismayed."
DEUTERONOMY 31:8 NKJV

Are there days when you are afraid of just about everything? When these days happen, remember that God loves you; and He will *always* be with you. He doesn't want you to fear a thing!

Dear God, please help me never to forget that You go before me—You know all that I am doing and all that will happen to me.

MORNING

Running on Empty

I have observed something else under the sun. The fastest runner doesn't always win the race, and the strongest warrior doesn't always win the battle.
ECCLESIASTES 9:11 NLT

Are you trying too hard? Always rushing here and there, involving yourself in a dozen things? Has keeping up appearances become an issue? Watch out. Before long, you might be running on empty.

Lord, I'm so tired! I've taken on too much. My heart was in the right place, but somewhere along the way I got off track. Redirect me, Father. Show me what to give up and what to stick with. Amen.

EVENING

Got Bling?

The twelve gates were twelve pearls, each gate made of a single pearl. The great street of the city was of gold, as pure as transparent glass.
REVELATION 21:21 NIV

God has created a place for us to go after we leave the earth, and He wants you to have more there than you will ever have here. He wants your eternal home to be the best of the best! The next time you put on your bling, think about how it's only a taste of what is yet to come!

God, thank You for creating my beautiful, heavenly home. I love Your bling! Amen.

DAY
96

MORNING

The Rainbow

"I have set my rainbow in the clouds, and it will be the sign of the covenant between me and the earth."
GENESIS 9:13 NIV

Every day God freely displays His blessings. Are we too busy or disinterested to appreciate their wonder? Even if we've forgotten He's there, reminders are all around, for He is the God of covenants. In a world where promises (or covenants) are disregarded routinely, I need God's kind of stability.

Lord, only You can renew my weary spirit and fill me with fresh expectation. Keep my eyes on Your rainbows!

EVENING

Hello? You There?

He has never let you down, never looked the other way when you were being kicked around. He has never wandered off to do his own thing; he has been right there, listening.
PSALM 22:24 MSG

God promises that He is always there with us and that He will never change. Sometimes it's hard to believe that because we can't see Him. But we do hear His voice in our hearts when we pray, we feel His presence when someone offers comfort in His name, and we feel Him surrounding us when we praise Him.

Father, please show Yourself to me today.

MORNING

A Hospitable Heart

After [Lydia] was baptized, along with everyone in her household, she said in a surge of hospitality, "If you're confident that I'm in this with you and believe in the Master truly, come home with me and be my guests."
ACTS 16:15 MSG

You can follow Lydia's lead. Whether your home is small or large, you can choose to be hospitable. Invite a friend who needs a pick-me-up to join you for a meal during the week. If elderly neighbors are unable to get out, take your hospitality to them!

Father, give me a heart for hospitality.
May I always serve others in Your name. Amen.

EVENING

Do-Over

Count yourself lucky, how happy you must be—
you get a fresh start, your slate's wiped clean.
PSALM 32:1 MSG

In real life, we don't get many do-overs. Isn't it nice that with God we always get to start over? No matter what we've done, God still loves us and forgives us. With God, we always win!

Lord, thank You for forgiving my sins
and giving me a new beginning. Amen.

DAY
98

MORNING

Fearfully and Wonderfully Made

For You formed my inward parts;
You wove me in my mother's womb.
PSALM 139:13 NASB

Each of us has not only an inborn sense that there is a God, but also an understanding that we possess a designed intent. Your parents aren't responsible for your creation, God is. Had He not willed your very existence, you would not have happened. God wants to use your life to further His kingdom.

Lord, please renew my understanding that You created me in Your own image and likeness with a body, mind, and spirit.

EVENING

Father Knows Best

Your Father knoweth what things ye have need of.
MATTHEW 6:8 KJV

Before you pray for something, ask yourself if your desire is a godly one. If it is, then wait patiently to see what God will do. Remember that when you trust Him with your life, everything works out for the best.

Dear God, thank You for loving me enough to choose what's best for my life instead of spoiling me with what I want. Amen.

MORNING

Guilt-Free

*So now there is no condemnation
for those who belong to Christ Jesus.*
ROMANS 8:1 NLT

When we confess our failures, repent, and move on, God wipes those mistakes away—He sees the child He created, who is washed in the blood of Jesus.

Guilt has held back the blessings of God long enough! Let it go! Have faith in the blood that cleanses *all* sins—past, present, and future.

Father God, I thank You that You have forgiven me. Help me to forgive myself—and to let go of the guilt that keeps me from becoming the person You say that I am.

EVENING

Escaping Temptation

No temptation has overtaken you that is not common to man.
1 CORINTHIANS 10:13 ESV

The Bible says that you will be tempted. You'll be stuck in that moment when you know what you should do but pause to decide what you will actually do. It's in that split second that God wants you to know there is an escape—a right choice to make. He will be faithful in helping you to overcome it. Just look to Him!

*Dear Jesus, thank You that You will make
a way for me to get through anything.*

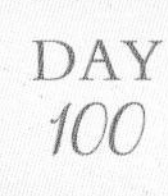

DAY 100

Morning

Tough Faith

These people of faith died not yet having in hand what was promised, but still believing.
HEBREWS 11:13 MSG

Most of us want to identify with the triumphant heroes listed in Hebrews 11, the "faith chapter." God protected them as they succeeded in doing great things for Him. We would rather forget others mentioned who did not achieve their goals during their lifetimes, suffering injustice and hardship. But God has not forgotten them.

Father, when I am sick and tired of doing good, help me to say good-bye to earthly expectations and wave hello to Your forever love. Amen.

Evening

Just Be You!

I praise you, for I am fearfully and wonderfully made. Wonderful are your works; my soul knows it very well.
PSALM 139:14 ESV

Take a few minutes and open your Bible. Read the rest of Psalm 139. Ask God to help you understand these verses and believe them. Print out the words and hang them on your wall or on your bathroom mirror as a special reminder that God made you to be *you*!

Dear God, thank You for the gifts and ideas that You have given me. Help me not to be afraid to be myself.

MORNING

Praise and Dance

Let everything that has breath praise the LORD. Praise the LORD!
PSALM 150:6 NASB

Whom are we to praise? The Lord! Where are we to praise? Wherever His congregation gathers. For what are we praising? For who He is, what He's done, and the way He's done it. How are we to praise? With our voices, our instruments, and our bodies as we dance in worship.

Lord, help me to yield my spirit up to You in true worship.

EVENING

Danger!

The LORD will watch over your coming and going both now and forevermore.
PSALM 121:8 NIV

The Bible doesn't guarantee us a perfect life here on earth. In fact, Jesus said we will have many troubles, but the Lord is right here with us. He may not sweep away every misery or heal every wound, but He has promised to give you strength to handle whatever life throws at you.

Jesus, help me to trust in You—that no matter what happens each day, I know You'll stay beside me, helping me with every choice I make and every step I take. Amen.

MORNING

She Gave, and He Gave Back

When he was come, they brought him into the upper chamber: and all the widows stood by him weeping, and shewing the coats and garments which Dorcas made, while she was with them.
ACTS 9:39 KJV

Dorcas had given her life to serve God, and God had given it back. When you give your life to serve others, you are honoring God—and finding life.

Lord Jesus, I don't understand why You would give Your life for me. Please strengthen me for this joyful task.

EVENING

God's Masterpiece

For we are God's masterpiece. He has created us anew in Christ Jesus, so we can do the good things he planned for us long ago.
EPHESIANS 2:10 NLT

We were created in order to bring glory to our Creator. When you begin to worry about your appearance or wonder if you have enough talent, remember. . .God made you to be just as you are. And you are His masterpiece!

Heavenly Father, I don't feel so special sometimes. Sometimes I feel quite ordinary. Help me to remember that I am beautiful in Your sight. I am Your masterpiece. Amen.

Morning

Infinite and Personal

Am I a God at hand, saith the Lord, and not a God afar off? . . .
Do not I fill heaven and earth?
Jeremiah 23:23–24 KJV

Whether your day is crumbling around you or is the best day you have ever had, do you see God in it? Whether we see Him or not, God tells us He is there. And He's here, too—in the good times and bad.

Lord, empower me to trust You when it's hard to remember that You are near. And help me to live thankfully when times are good. Amen.

Evening

You Can Do It!

"The Lord is my strength and my defense; he has become my salvation.
He is my God, and I will praise him, my father's God, and I will exalt him."
Exodus 15:2 NIV

Take a few minutes every day to spend time with God in prayer and worship. When you do, you'll find you really *can* do everything you need to do because God will give you the strength you need when you need it (Isaiah 40:31).

Dear God, thank You for being a loving
God who gives me strength. Amen.

DAY
104

MORNING

Known by God

But if anyone loves God, he is known by God.
1 CORINTHIANS 8:3 ESV

How do we show that we love God? Loving God is first and foremost a response to being known and loved by God. We can't muster emotion or feeling toward God, nor do we love Him simply by willing ourselves to acts of obedience. We begin to love God when we grasp what it means to be known by God.

Lord, renew my love for You. Help me to remember that You knew me and loved me before I ever knew You.

EVENING

The Wages of Sin

For the wages of sin is death, but the free gift of God is eternal life in Christ Jesus our Lord.
ROMANS 6:23 NASB

Jesus persevered everything—because He loves the world and everyone in it (John 3:16). He extended His grace to *everyone* so we can have hope for a future of *everlasting* bliss where we can worship Him and live to the *absolute* fullest.

Father, I can't comprehend why You sent Jesus to die for me. I can't even begin to imagine what it was like. But thank You. With everything in me. In Jesus' name I pray. Amen.

Morning

Taxes Must Be Paid

Every person is to be in subjection to the governing authorities. For there is no authority except from God, and those which exist are established by God. . . . For because of this you also pay taxes, for rulers are servants of God, devoting themselves to this very thing.
Romans 13:1, 6 NASB

We're following scripture. . .we're supporting a government that God has truly blessed.

Lord, let me give to the government not grudgingly but out of obedience to You. And please assist those in authority over me to direct wisely the use of these funds.

Evening

Surround Yourself with the Word

He gives strength to the weary and increases the power of the weak.
Isaiah 40:29 NIV

Do you need to be strengthened today? Reach for your Bible and swallow down as much as you can! Write your favorite verses down on pieces of paper and put them on your bathroom mirror. Memorize them and say them out loud.

God, sometimes I don't even want to get out of bed in the morning. Thank You for giving me the strength to keep going, even when I really want to pull the covers over my head! Amen.

DAY
106

Morning

Cabbage Patch Love

The Lord said, "I have loved you."
But you ask, "How have you loved us?"
Malachi 1:2 NCV

When we examine the facts, it's obvious that God loves us. He longs for us to love Him back. Let's open our eyes—and hearts—to that perfect love.

Father, You chose us to be Your own. You love us with all the tender compassion of a doting Father. Let us rest in Your love.

Evening

Learn to Use Your Sword

Study to shew thyself approved unto God, a workman that needeth not to be ashamed, rightly dividing the word of truth.
2 Timothy 2:15 KJV

The sword—is the sword of the Spirit, which is the Word of God. We need to be studying the Word, hiding it in our hearts, so that we are ready to use it when God calls us to.

Lord, I want to study Your Word so that I can be prepared to serve You better each day. I want to be a worker who has no need to be ashamed. Amen.

Morning

Comforting Close

The Lord is close to the brokenhearted;
he rescues those whose spirits are crushed.
Psalm 34:18 NLT

When others turn away from us, we know we can always rely on our eternal Father, the One who will never leave or forsake us. He is close to us in the best and the worst of times. Take His hand. Rest in His arms. Let Him love you.

God, thank You for always being there. Heal my broken heart, my crushed spirit. With every breath I take, may I know You are right here beside me, loving me. Amen.

Evening

A Hopeful Tomorrow

Why are you cast down, O my soul? And why are you disquieted within me?
Hope in God, for I shall yet praise Him for the help of His countenance.
Psalm 42:5 NKJV

God will always give you new hope for a new day. After all, He gave each one of us the hope of eternal life in heaven with Him through His precious Son, our Savior. How can we have a down day when we think of that?

Dear God, please help me to get past this down feeling
and be able to hope again like I did this morning. Amen.

DAY
108

MORNING

No Worries

"So don't worry about tomorrow, for tomorrow will bring its own worries. Today's trouble is enough for today."
MATTHEW 6:34 NLT

Today, trust Jesus' assurance that He will take care of you. Ask Him to help you let go of your worrying nature and replace it with a spirit of praise and thanksgiving. It won't happen overnight, but soon you'll feel the true freedom from worry that only Jesus can supply.

Jesus, help me to place all my concerns in Your capable hands so that I can be free to praise You as You deserve!

EVENING

Does God Like Me?

"The LORD your God is with you, the Mighty Warrior who saves. He will take great delight in you; in his love he will no longer rebuke you, but will rejoice over you with singing."
ZEPHANIAH 3:17 NIV

When you come to know Jesus as your Savior, God washes all your sins away and He sees you as the perfect girl you are. And you can say with confidence, "God likes me!" You are liked. You are loved. You are His!

Dear God, thank You for loving me. . . and for liking me just the way I am.

Morning

Chosen

Before I formed you in the womb I knew [and] approved of you [as My chosen instrument], and before you were born I separated and set you apart, consecrating you.
Jeremiah 1:5 AMP

Nothing about us or our circumstances surprises God. He knew about everything before we were born. And He equipped us for every trial and difficulty we will ever face in life. What an awesome God we serve!

Father, the thought that You chose me before the foundation of the world and set me apart for a specific calling is humbling. May I go forward with a renewed purpose in life.

Evening

Your Heavenly Father

See what great love the Father has lavished on us, that we should be called children of God!
1 John 3:1 NIV

God enjoys celebrating your life as much as you do. He takes pride in all you do and say. . .in your adventures and how you handle your challenges. He doesn't even care if you're the one in one of your old school yearbooks with bed head. You are His treasure!

God, I celebrate life with You and plan to make the best of today. May all I do and say be pleasing to You. Amen.

DAY
110

Morning

Encounter at the Well

There came a woman of Samaria to draw water.
Jesus said to her, "Give Me a drink."
JOHN 4:7 NASB

Here lived a woman of ill repute. Her presence at the well late in the afternoon was an acknowledgment that she didn't fit in. Jesus Christ went right to the heart of her problem: He explained the process of eternal life to her, and she was transformed.

Father, help me to seek out those who for whatever reason are shunned and despised. They need You so much.

Evening

Changed Plans

"For I know the plans I have for you," declares the LORD,
"plans to prosper you and not to harm you, plans to give you hope and a future."
JEREMIAH 29:11 NIV

There are days when you don't know where you are going or what you are doing with your life. It's so easy to believe that you have to decide everything for yourself. But remember, your heavenly Father has a plan in place.

God, I know You have plans for me—and Your plans aren't always my plans. And thanks for always understanding how I feel. Amen.

MORNING

The Forever Word

"The grass withers and the flowers fall,
but the word of our God endures forever."
ISAIAH 40:8 NIV

When we study God's Word wholeheartedly, He will illuminate it, giving us an understanding that brings perfect peace. While everything around us changes, we can rest in the one thing that stands forever—the true, unchanging Word of God.

Lord Jesus, I thank You for Your Word. I pray that You would teach me more and more how to obtain its nourishment and wisdom for my spirit. I ask You to bless me with great understanding.

EVENING

Here's How God Sees You

So Peter went over the side of the boat and walked on the water toward Jesus.
But when he saw the strong wind and the waves,
he was terrified and began to sink.
MATTHEW 14:29–30 NLT

When you take your eyes off Jesus—just like Peter—your self-image will begin to sink. Your faith will grow weak. But when you keep your eyes on Christ, you'll begin to see yourself as He sees you!

God, help me to keep my eyes on You so that I can see myself just as You see me.

DAY 112

Morning

One Day at a Time

Blessed be the Lord, who daily loadeth us with benefits, even the God of our salvation.
Psalm 68:19 KJV

God gives us blessings every day so that we still have what we need after we have spent ourselves on life's disappointments.

Father, You give us bread daily. We praise You for Your constant care and ask that You will train our eyes to focus on Your blessings, not on our failings. Amen.

Evening

Where's Your Playbook?

All Scripture is inspired by God and is useful to teach us what is true and to make us realize what is wrong in our lives.
2 Timothy 3:16 NLT

Take a few minutes each day to read God's Word. It will guide you, play by play, to be the best at whatever He has planned for your life.

Jesus, thank You for being my coach. I know I can win in the game of life with Your encouraging guidebook. Amen.

MORNING

Turn Your Ear to Wisdom

For the LORD gives wisdom; from His mouth
come knowledge and understanding.
PROVERBS 2:6 NASB

God's Word says wisdom is truly a gift since it comes from the mouth of God, from the very words He speaks. And all God's words have been written down for us, through the inspiration of the Holy Spirit.

Know that if you hold fast to the precepts contained in the Bible, you will walk in integrity. Instead of gravitating toward potholes, your feet will be planted on the straight and narrow road.

Lord, help me to walk in wisdom every day.

EVENING

God Said It, and He Meant It

He who began a good work in you will carry
it on to completion until the day of Christ Jesus.
PHILIPPIANS 1:6 NIV

God said that when you turned to Him, He gave you a new identity. You are a new person in Christ. He doesn't play games with that. He is not a liar. He promises that He'll finish the work He started in you. You can trust Him.

Dear God, help me remember Your promises and know that I am a new creation in You, and no one can take that away from me. Amen.

DAY 114

Morning

A Little Time with God

"I thank You and praise You, O God of my fathers;
You have given me wisdom and might."
DANIEL 2:23 NKJV

God blesses us every day in both great and simple ways. Children, friends, work, faith—all these things form a bountiful buffet of gifts, and caring for them isn't always enough. We need to spend a little time with the One who has granted us the blessings.

Father God, You have given us so much to be grateful for. Show me a way to spend more time with You, and help me to grow closer and know You better. Amen.

Evening

My Life GPS

For we are His workmanship, created in Christ Jesus for good works,
which God prepared beforehand so that we would walk in them.
EPHESIANS 2:10 NASB

God is our GPS. He sees the whole picture. He knows every detail of every life. His children are referred to as His "workmanship" in the Bible. You were made to love Him and to do good works that only you can do!

Dear Father, help me to listen to You and to obey You so that I can do the works You have created me to do. In Jesus' name, amen.

MORNING

Healed Miraculously

There is in Jerusalem by the sheep gate a pool. . . . In these lay a multitude of those who were sick, blind, lame, and withered, [waiting for the moving of the waters; for an angel of the Lord went down at certain seasons into the pool and stirred up the water; whoever then first, after the stirring up of the water, stepped in was made well from whatever disease with which he was afflicted.]
JOHN 5:2–4 NASB

Do you honestly desire to rid yourself of the things which debilitate? True healing of our souls requires a change of direction.

Lord, if sin is at the root of my infirmity,
then bring me to swift repentance.

EVENING

The Favor Factor

Surely, LORD, you bless the righteous;
you surround them with your favor as with a shield.
PSALM 5:12 NIV

Start thanking God for His supernatural favor. It's amazing, really. Once you start praising God for His supernatural favor, you'll begin to see more of it in your life. So start praying and praising, and enjoy the favor of God today!

Lord, thank You for Your favor. Amen.

DAY 116

Morning

Lend a Hand

"What do you think? Which of the three became a neighbor to the man attacked by robbers?" "The one who treated him kindly," the religion scholar responded. Jesus said, "Go and do the same."
LUKE 10:36–37 MSG

While it's good to be cautious, the parable of the good Samaritan tells us to help one another. Not only does becoming involved provide someone needed assistance, but it expands our heart reach. We become Jesus to others, spreading love and kindness, increasing our witness.

Father, thank You for Your loving-kindness.
Give me an opening to share Your love with others. Amen.

Evening

A True Friend Will Tell You the Truth

"No longer do I call you servants, for the servant does not know what his master is doing; but I have called you friends, for all that I have heard from my Father I have made known to you."
JOHN 15:15 ESV

If you want a friend who will tell you the truth and help you if you are going the wrong way, Jesus is this kind of friend. He loves you more than anyone can. Just open your heart to hear Him.

Lord, thank You that there is no one more faithful.

Morning

Sleep on It

It is of the Lord's mercies that we are not consumed, because his compassions fail not. They are new every morning: great is thy faithfulness.
Lamentations 3:22–23 KJV

Through the never-ending compassion of God, His faithfulness is revealed afresh each morning. We can rise with renewed vigor. We can eagerly anticipate the new day, leaving behind the concerns of yesterday.

Heavenly Father, thank You for giving me a new measure of Your mercy and compassion each day so that my concerns don't consume me. I rest in You and I lay my burdens at Your feet.

Evening

Which Road Should I Take?

"I say this because I know what I am planning for you," says the Lord. "I have good plans for you, not plans to hurt you. I will give you hope and a good future."
Jeremiah 29:11 NCV

Did you know that God has a spiritual road map for your life? The Bible gives you all the directions you need. When you come to a fork in the road—and you don't know which way to take—His Word will give you answers. Just listen closely to His still, small voice.

God, thank You for helping me choose the right road!

DAY
118

MORNING

Our Refuge in Time of Pain

Be gracious to me, O God. . .
for my soul takes refuge in You.
PSALM 57:1 NASB

When the world around you breaks loose, don't lose your hold on God. And rest assured, He won't let go of you.

Father, thank You for Your words of comfort when I am wracked with grief and pain. Help me to never forget that You are there for me.

EVENING

Happiness versus Joy

But let all who take refuge in you rejoice; let them sing
joyful praises forever. Spread your protection over them,
that all who love your name may be filled with joy.
PSALM 5:11 NLT

Even on your most difficult days, spend some time in prayer or worshipping the Lord, and you will feel that deep-down joy well up in your heart. Try it!

Thank You, God, for planting joy deep down in my heart! May others be pointed to You when they see my joy bubbling up, even in hard times. Amen.

MORNING

Unremarkable Lives

Then Jephthah the Gileadite died and was buried in one of the cities of Gilead. Now Ibzan of Bethlehem judged Israel after him. . . . And he judged Israel seven years. Then Ibzan died and was buried in Bethlehem.
JUDGES 12:7–10 NASB

How can we discern the will of God for our lives and avoid living an unremarkable life? Daily prayer is definitely the main source. And this involves not only relating our needs to God but also listening for His directions. For He never meant for us to traverse through this maze called life without the road maps He would supply.

Lord, remind me to linger in prayer, listening for Your voice.

EVENING

A Loved Child of God

For you are all one in Christ Jesus.
GALATIANS 3:28 NLT

When you start feeling down, remember how much God loves you. The Bible tells us that His love is unfailing! Psalm 13:5 says, "But I trust in your unfailing love; my heart rejoices in your salvation" (NIV). That's a good verse to memorize for those days when you're feeling bad about yourself. Never forget that you're a child of God and you're loved!

God, help me to remember that I am Your child and that You love me more than anyone else ever will. I rejoice in You!

Morning

The Blazing Furnace

"If we are thrown into the blazing furnace, the God we serve is able to deliver us from it, and he will deliver us from Your Majesty's hand."
Daniel 3:17 NIV

Too often we think that our faith should keep us out of the furnace: a health crisis, financial worries, troubling situations with our kids. But being in the furnace doesn't mean that God has abandoned us. As promised in Hebrews 13:5 (NKJV), "I will never leave you nor forsake you."

Lord God, thank You that I can count on You to be with me in every circumstance. Amen.

Evening

Dumpy Days

The Lord hath comforted his people.
Isaiah 49:13 KJV

The next time you're in a foul mood that you can't seem to snap out of, take some time to pray. Grab a box of tissues and sneak away to a private place where you can talk to God, out loud, without being interrupted or overheard. Tell Him everything that's troubling you, and ask Him to fill you with His comfort. You'll be amazed at how much better you feel.

Lord, I'm so glad that You understand me even when I don't understand myself.

MORNING

It's Not My Fault

Someone who lives on milk is still an infant
and doesn't know how to do what is right.
HEBREWS 5:13 NLT

Are you using the shortcomings of someone else to justify your own actions? Take a moment to ask God to examine your heart in this important area.

Lord, as hard as it is to admit when I am wrong,
teach me to humbly accept responsibility for my choices.
I pray for growth and maturity in my Christian walk. Amen.

EVENING

Promises Kept

The believer replied, "Every promise of God proves true;
he protects everyone who runs to him for help."
PROVERBS 30:5 MSG

God keeps His promises *always*. He cannot break them any more than He can lie. He is God, and He never breaks His word. His promises are true for those who lived long ago, all the way up to the present, and even into the future. Trust Him. Run to Him!

Dear God, please help me to remember that You always
keep Your promises, that You will guide and protect me.

DAY 122

Morning

Anna, the Prophetess

And there was a prophetess, Anna the daughter of Phanuel, of the tribe of Asher. . . . She never left the temple, serving night and day with fastings and prayer.
Luke 2:36–37 NASB

God had promised Anna that she would see the Messiah before she died. She waited eighty-four years, biding her time in service to the Lord. And He kept His Word. Let us strive to follow Anna's prayerful example, and we, too, will be blessed by God.

Lord, call my heart to faithfulness and prayer.
May I serve as an example to encourage others.

Evening

Better Than Happy

In him our hearts rejoice, for we trust in his holy name.
Psalm 33:21 NIV

When things seem to be out of control, just know that God is at work in ways you can't see. You don't have to be happy about the troubles in your life, but trusting God can give you joy in spite of them.

Dear God, thank You for the joy that comes from knowing You.
Sometimes my life doesn't go the way I'd like it to, but I know
that I can trust You to help me through even the toughest times.

Morning

Time for Praise

And a voice came from the throne, saying, "Give praise to our God, all you His bond-servants, you who fear Him, the small and the great."
Revelation 19:5 NASB

The more we praise God, the more we will feel the joy of His presence in the ordinary moments of our day-to-day lives.

Jesus, You are worthy to be praised; help me to make praising Your name a lifelong habit. Amen.

Evening

The Fingerprints of God

For You formed my inward parts;
You wove me in my mother's womb.
Psalm 139:13 NASB

You're not only God's uniquely made child but also created in His image (Genesis 1:27)! God doesn't make mistakes. "God saw *all* that He had made, and behold, it was *very* good" (Genesis 1:31 NASB, emphasis added).

Lord, thank You for creating me as I am. Thank You for loving me no matter how sinful I am or how ugly I may feel. Thanks for Your unending and magnificent love. In Jesus' name I pray. Amen.

MORNING

God in the Details

"When we heard of it, our hearts melted in fear and everyone's courage failed because of you, for the LORD your God is God in heaven above and on the earth below."
JOSHUA 2:11 NIV

Just as the Lord cares for the tiniest bird (Matthew 10:29–31), so He seeks to be a part of every detail in your life. Look for Him there.

Father God, I know You are by my side every day, good or bad, and that You love and care for me.

EVENING

Down in the Dumps

Be full of joy always because you belong to the Lord. Again I say, be full of joy!
PHILIPPIANS 4:4 NLV

God is watching over you; He will forgive your sins; and He has prepared a special place for you in heaven. What amazing things to be joyful about! If you trust God to do these things for you, He can help you climb out of the pit and view the day with fresh eyes and a happy heart.

God, thank You for giving me so much to be joyful about.

MORNING

Appreciate What You Have

"You shall not covet your neighbor's house; you shall not covet your neighbor's wife, nor his male servant, nor his female servant, nor his ox, nor his donkey, nor anything that is your neighbor's."
EXODUS 20:17 NKJV

When God tells us that we "shall not," we must pay attention. Catch yourself when you sense a desire for that which is not yours. Appreciate your own gifts, blessings, and belongings.

God, You have poured out so many blessings on me. Protect my heart from desiring that which belongs to others. Amen.

EVENING

What Makes You Stumble?

"Jeremiah, say to the people, 'This is what the LORD says: When people fall down, don't they get up again? When they discover they're on the wrong road, don't they turn back?'"
JEREMIAH 8:4 NLT

We worry about the big stuff—the things we know for sure are not right for us. But if we don't pay attention to the "little" bad choices we make, pretty soon they will become mountains that block our view of God. Always choose well in the little things, and the big decisions will be easier.

Dear Lord, thank You for guiding me each step of the way. Amen.

DAY
126

Morning

Search for Happiness

I explored with my mind how to stimulate my body with wine while my mind was guiding me wisely.
Ecclesiastes 2:3 NASB

Solomon explored with his mind how to stimulate his body. Then he enlarged his empire, built houses, planted vineyards, made gardens and parks, engineered ponds of water to irrigate a forest, bought male and female slaves, flocks, and herds, and collected silver and gold. But did any of this bring him true happiness?

Lord, help me not to be drawn away from You by the endless pursuit of things. Instead, I desire Your presence, guidance, and wisdom.

Evening

In the Middle of the Mess

Can anything ever separate us from Christ's love? Does it mean he no longer loves us if we have trouble or calamity, or are persecuted, or hungry, or destitute, or in danger, or threatened with death?
Romans 8:35 NLT

When bad stuff happens, God has already made His choice to stick with you; but you have to make the choice to stick with Him.

God, I don't understand why some things happen, but I promise to look for Your love in the middle of the messes. Amen.

MORNING

So, Talk!

No one is able to come to Me unless the Father Who sent Me attracts and draws him and gives him the desire to come to Me.
JOHN 6:44 AMP

Our Father always wants to talk. In fact, the very impulse to pray originates in God. In his book *The Pursuit of God*, author A. W. Tozer writes, "We pursue God because, and only because, He has first put an urge within us that spurs us to the pursuit."

Today, Lord, I give You praise, honor and glory—
and my heart's deepest longings.

EVENING

Don't Believe the Bully

The LORD is on my side; I will not fear. What can man do to me?
PSALM 118:6 ESV

Hurting people hurt people. More often than not, a "mean girl" has had a lot of hurts in her life and hasn't yet experienced the love of Jesus. You might not be the one to give bullies the help they need, but you can pray for them whenever they come to mind.

Dear God, help me to have patience
with the difficult people in my life.

DAY
128

MORNING

Practicality versus Passion

Leaving her water jar, the woman went back to the town and said to the people,
"Come, see a man who told me everything I ever did.
Could this be the Messiah?"
JOHN 4:28–29 NIV

Do you live with such passion, or do you cling to your water jar? Has an encounter with Christ made an impact that cannot be denied in your life?

Lord, help me to lay down anything that stifles my passion for sharing the Good News with others. Amen.

EVENING

My Lord Knows Me Better Than Myself

Even before there is a word on my tongue, behold, O LORD, You know it all.
PSALM 139:4 NASB

God knows everything about you. The good, the bad, and even the ugly. But you know what? He loves you, flaws and all. He won't ever turn His back on you; He'll always be there.

God, thank You for being my best friend. Even when others fail me, You'll always be there. Help me to be Your light to others. Amen.

Morning

Remembering

"Behold, I have engraved you on the palms of my hands;
your walls are continually before me."
Isaiah 49:16 ESV

Romans 8:34 (NIV) says, "Christ Jesus, who died—more than that, who was raised to life—is at the right hand of God and is also interceding for us." Jesus is remembering us in constant prayer to the Father. His eyes never close and His memory never fails. God remembers us.

Father, thank You that through Christ You have brought me to Yourself, You reign over my life, and You always remember me.

Evening

Take a Deep Breath!

Though you have made me see troubles, many and bitter, you will restore my life again; from the depths of the earth you will again bring me up.
Psalm 71:20 NIV

Take a deep breath. God made you—and He wants to fill your heart with joy. He knows everyone will have a bad day from time to time. Just remember that He made you with power, love, and a sound mind. Then thank Him for it!

Lord, tomorrow is a new day. Thank You for fresh starts! Amen.

DAY 130

Morning

Jesus, Bread of Life

"As the living Father sent Me, and I live because of the Father, so he who eats Me, he also will live because of Me. This is the bread which came down out of heaven; not as the fathers ate and died; he who eats this bread will live forever."

John 6:57–58 NASB

To truly partake of Christ is to accept Him as He is, fully God and fully man, sent from God, recognizing our need for Him. What is your response?

Lord, when I don't understand the scriptures,
Your Holy Spirit will provide me with comprehension.

Evening

Fake It till You Make It

Create in me a clean heart, O God,
and renew a steadfast spirit within me.

Psalm 51:10 NASB

If you want to be pure and righteous on the outside, you need to be pure and righteous on the inside. That's what it means to be true to yourself and honor God.

Dear God, please forgive me for the things I do that are
not like Jesus. Help me to walk in truth today and always.

Morning

Timely Words

The Lord God gives me the
right words to encourage the weary.
Isaiah 50:4 CEV

God has given us tongues and fingers to communicate timely words to the weary around us. Perhaps it is time to send a card through the mail or to pick up the phone and call a friend you haven't seen for a while. When God prompts us to speak, we become part of His answer.

Lord God, You have given us gifts that can lift up the weary when they most need it. Teach us to listen for Your instructions. Amen.

Evening

Love One Another

"So now I am giving you a new commandment: Love each other. Just as I have loved you, you should love each other. Your love for one another will prove to the world that you are my disciples."
John 13:34–35 NLT

Treat others with kindness—*always*. You will be known as a Christian when you show love, just as the Savior first loved you.

Jesus, I want to be loving, but often I fail. It's so hard to put others before myself. Help me, Lord. Amen.

DAY 132

Morning

Samuel Is Born

It came about in due time, after Hannah had conceived, that she gave birth to a son; and she named him Samuel, saying, "Because I have asked him of the Lord."
1 Samuel 1:20 NASB

God was now training Samuel to take over as judge of Israel, as Eli's own sons had no regard for the Lord. As Samuel continued to grow "in favor with the Lord" (1 Samuel 2:26 NIV), the Lord declared, "Those who honor me I will honor, but those who despise me will be disdained" (1 Samuel 2:30 NIV).

Lord, if You should give me a child, guide me as You guided Hannah—to sincere faithfulness.

Evening

Do You Feel Inadequate?

"I will strengthen you and help you; I will uphold you with my righteous right hand."
Isaiah 41:10 NIV

Has God placed a dream in your heart? When you think about your dream, do you feel excited? Or do you feel like you can't do it? If you feel like you are unable, be encouraged! It's actually great that you know you can't do it all on your own, because then you know that you have to lean on God to help you.

Lord, thank You that You give me strength to accomplish the dreams You have for me.

MORNING

God in Disguise

"And the King will say, 'I tell you the truth, when you did it to one of the least of these my brothers and sisters, you were doing it to me!' "
MATTHEW 25:40 NLT

Sometimes we can become so concerned with serving God that we forget that God is served when we serve people. Just as it is possible to have head knowledge *about* God without having a relationship *with* God, so can people interact with others without ever meeting a person's real need.

Lord, open my eyes to see those who need care. Amen.

EVENING

Ready and Waiting

Don't worry about anything; instead, pray about everything. Tell God what you need, and thank him for all he has done.
PHILIPPIANS 4:6 NLT

God is ready to listen anytime. The instruction we have is not to worry but rather pray. He will hear you and will give you what you need.

Dear heavenly Father, thank You for listening to me right now and for always being ready to listen. You're never too busy or too distracted to give me Your attention. Thank You for all You have done. Amen.

DAY
134

Morning

Rock of Ages

So trust in the Lord (commit yourself to Him, lean on Him, hope confidently in Him) forever; for the Lord God is an everlasting Rock [the Rock of Ages].
Isaiah 26:4 AMP

You and I can have peace. Authentic peace. God-breathed peace. Not because we live in some make-believe world, repeating positive-thinking statements in an attempt to alter reality. Not because we've been able to avoid adversity or opposition. No, we can have peace simply and only because we trust our heavenly Father.

Father God, grant me the ability to trust You, come what may.

Evening

Hello God. . .Are You There?

The Lord is near to all who call on Him, to all who call on Him in truth.
Psalm 145:18 NLV

Not only does the Lord hear you, but He cares about what you're telling Him. He's on your side. So next time you really wish someone would listen to you, forget about calling a friend on the phone. Call on the best Friend of all, the one who's always there when you need Him.

God, I'm so glad You hear my prayers!
You're always there for me, ready to listen.

MORNING

Not Even His Brothers Believed

"If You do these things, show Yourself to the world." For not even His brothers were believing in Him.
JOHN 7:4–5 NASB

Jesus tells them, "My time is not yet here, but your time is always opportune. . . . Go up to the feast yourselves; I do not go up to this feast because My time has not yet fully come" (John 7:6, 8 NASB). After his brothers left, Christ went secretly to the feast.

Thank You, Jesus, for reminding me to wait for God's timing in my life, especially when the pressure applied by others would have me rush on ahead.

EVENING

Courageous

Be strong, and let your heart take courage, all you who wait for the LORD!
PSALM 31:24 ESV

But God doesn't want us to feel afraid. When we place our trust in Him, He gives us courage. No matter what we may face, God wants to face it with us. He will never leave us alone, and if we ask Him to help us, He will. We just have to hold our heads high and trust Him.

Dear Father, thank You for giving me courage to face whatever may come.

DAY
136

Morning

The Gift of Receiving

"It is more blessed to give than to receive."
Acts 20:35 NIV

Are you trying to keep a stiff upper lip to show the world how strong you are? Maybe you are fully capable of succeeding with no outside help. But in doing so, you might rob others of the joy of giving.

Lord, please give me the wisdom and the grace to know when to accept help from others—and even the courage to ask for it when I need it.

Evening

Do You Really Love God?

If anyone boasts, "I love God," and goes right on hating his brother or sister, thinking nothing of it, he is a liar. If he won't love the person he can see, how can he love the God he can't see? The command we have from Christ is blunt: Loving God includes loving people. You've got to love both.
1 John 4:20–21 MSG

Are you struggling to be nice to someone else? Ask God for help.

God, please forgive me for my anger.

MORNING

Church

And let us not neglect our meeting together, as some people do, but encourage one another, especially now that the day of his return is drawing near.
HEBREWS 10:25 NLT

Believers are strengthened as we focus on the Lord together. Being reminded of God's truth is crucial. Fellowship encourages us in our spiritual walk. We've each been given at least one spiritual gift to benefit the church body, and that gift is exercised as we are connected to each other.

*Dear Lord, I need to worship You with other believers.
Help me to be consistent in church attendance. Amen.*

EVENING

Say What?

*"Love your enemies, do good to those who hate you,
bless those who curse you, pray for those who mistreat you."*
LUKE 6:27–28 NIV

So the next time someone acts ugly toward you, don't fight back. Instead, pray for her. You probably won't feel like praying for her at that very moment, but do it anyway. You may have to do it through gritted teeth, but if you'll do your part, God will do His.

God, please help me to love my enemies the same way You do. Amen.

DAY
138

Morning

Burden Bearing

"For I satisfy the weary ones and
refresh everyone who languishes."
Jeremiah 31:25 NASB

The promised result is God's rest—His peace, His refreshing of our spirits—in spite of any problem we face. When we submit to His yoke, we find that the burden truly is light and easy to bear. No longer languishing, we find ourselves refreshed, walking forward in His strength.

Father God, may we heed Jesus' invitation today, knowing that Your desire is to do all things for our good and Your glory.

Evening

All Wrapped Up

"God blesses those who mourn,
for they will be comforted."
Matthew 5:4 NLT

We need even more comfort when we are sad. When someone dies or a bad thing happens, God is ready to give us peace like a warm, fuzzy blanket. He comforts us like no one or nothing else can. The next time you need comfort, run to the heavenly Father and let Him wrap you up in His loving embrace.

Dear God, thank You for sending Your comfort just when I need it most. Help me to be a comfort to others, too. Amen.

Morning

Your Will Be Done

"Your kingdom come, your will be done, on earth as it is in heaven."
Matthew 6:10 NIV

We must trust that God's ways are higher than ours. We must believe that His will is perfect. We must hold fast to His love. As we do, He imparts peace to our hearts, and we are able to say with conviction, "Your will be done."

Dear Lord, may I rest secure in Your unconditional love. Enable me to trust You more. May I desire that Your will be done in my life. Amen.

Evening

Dreaming of Paradise

"What no eye has seen, nor ear heard, nor the heart of man imagined, what God has prepared for those who love him."
1 Corinthians 2:9 ESV

God has promised heaven to those who love and serve Him. Are you ready to go there? Now would be a great time to search your heart and make sure.

Lord, I don't know what heaven will be like, but I know I want to spend eternity there. Guide me through this life, and prepare me to meet You someday. Amen.

Morning

A Time to Mourn

There is an appointed time for everything. And there is a time for every event under heaven. . . . A time to weep and a time to laugh; a time to mourn and a time to dance.
Ecclesiastes 3:1, 4 NASB

Occasionally a time of mourning enters our lives, sometimes stealing in almost silently, sometimes brashly breaking down the door to our well-constructed sense of security. But tragedy and mourning are both part of the ebb and flow or "rhythm of life."

Lord, through my veil of tears help me to view Your rescuing hand, that I might reach out to grasp You more firmly.

Evening

Is Anyone There?

The Lord hears when I call to Him.
Psalm 4:3 NASB

God's always available. Day or night. Twenty-four hours, every day of the year, He never takes a vacation. And you can rest assured that He always hears us. The Bible is full of verses that back that up. He made you, He cares about you, and the coolest part? He's just waiting for you to call on Him. He longs to hear from you.

God, thank You for always listening. And remind me to keep the communication lines open, all day. Amen.

Morning

Keeping On

Blessed is the one who perseveres.
James 1:12 NIV

Perseverance means staying in the fight and refusing to give up. This attitude empowers us and makes the victim mentality dissipate. It builds confidence, one fight at a time. Keep on keeping on—it's a powerful life tool.

Lord, give me the strength to get up from the mat and continue. I choose to believe in Your promises. Amen.

Evening

En Garde! (On Your Guard!)

I have hidden your word in my heart that I might not sin against you. . . . I delight in your decrees; I will not neglect your word.
Psalm 119:11, 16 NIV

Reading God's Word daily is like practicing your fighting skills. As you hide His Word in your heart, you'll find yourself growing stronger in your faith. When the enemy tries to tempt you, you'll have no trouble holding him off because your sword of the Spirit will be ready. *En garde!*

Dear God, I am so thankful that You have given me Your Word as a powerful weapon. Amen.

DAY
142

Morning

But Even If

"If we are thrown into the blazing furnace,
the God whom we serve is able to save us."
Daniel 3:17 NLT

We need to be so grounded in the Word of God that we know His truth and trust Him above all else. Regardless of the circumstances or the temptations to disobey, we can stand firm in our faith in God's ability to rescue us from all situations.

Heavenly Father, I trust You no matter what and will obey Your Word. Help me stand in faith and face any fiery furnace that comes my way.

Evening

A Whole Pile of Birthday Presents

For you created my inmost being;
you knit me together in my mother's womb.
Psalm 139:13 NIV

God knows your happiest day and your darkest fear. The things that make you cry when you're all alone or the things that make you smile or laugh out loud. He knows your innermost secrets and your biggest dreams.

Lord, thank You that You know me inside and out. Thank You for loving me enough to help me become all that You created me to be. Amen.

MORNING

Wonderful Plans

LORD, you are my God; I will exalt you and praise your name, for in perfect faithfulness you have done wonderful things, things planned long ago.
ISAIAH 25:1 NIV

Recount and record God's faithfulness in your life in the past, because He has already demonstrated His wonderful plans to you in so many ways. You will find God to be faithful in the smallest aspects of your life and oh so worthy of your trust.

Oh Lord, help me to recount Your faithfulness, record Your faithfulness, and trust Your faithfulness in the future.

EVENING

A Sneak Peek

You are my hiding place and my shield; I hope in your word.
PSALM 119:114 ESV

When the Bible begins to seem dull or unimportant, just remember that it is God desiring to comfort, teach, and connect with you through His words.

God, thank You for giving me a sneak peek into Your character and promises. Please help me learn how to study and understand Your Word. Amen.

DAY 144

Morning

The Well-Stocked Purse

We can make our plans,
but the Lord determines our steps.
Proverbs 16:9 NLT

Only God knows what tomorrow will bring, and only He knows the tools we will need to get through any given situation. No packet of tissues or pocket-size scissors are going to be more useful than a spirit that is calm and trusts in the Lord.

Lord, help me to carry a peace-filled spirit with me at all times, and I will trust You to guide me and to provide for my needs along any path You may take me.

Evening

Even What You Don't Say

For God is greater than our worried hearts
and knows more about us than we do ourselves.
1 John 3:20 MSG

God spent the entire time you were in your mother's womb molding and shaping you, right down to the number of hairs on your head. It's more than okay for you to sit down with Him and say, "Father, I feel insecure and I don't know why. Can You show me?" Trust the One who made you to help you sort it out.

God, thank You for understanding who I am. I'm grateful
I can come to You when I don't have answers. Amen.

Morning

Beans or Steak?

Each of you must bring a gift in proportion to
the way the Lord your God has blessed you.
Deuteronomy 16:17 niv

No matter what our circumstances, God is blessing us—if we're following Him with steadfastness. Let's bless Him in return with our thanksgiving.

Lord, I thank You for the many blessings You give.
In exchange, I offer You the gift of my heart and life.

Evening

Don't Be Greedy, Help the Needy!

Use your hands for good hard work,
and then give generously to others in need.
Ephesians 4:28 nlt

Christmas is a time when churches sponsor clothing and food drives, and that's great. But the same recipients have needs all year long. Call your church and find out how you can help the needy in your community.

Dear God, please give me Your eyes
to see the needs in my community.

DAY
146

Morning

Where Did Sunday Go?

Then God blessed the seventh day and made it holy,
because on it he rested from all the work of creating that he had done.
Genesis 2:3 NIV

"Then God blessed the seventh day and made it holy," the Bible says. *If God rested on that day, shouldn't I?* Kate wondered. And if it was meant to be a blessed day, was Kate missing something God had in store for her?

Lord, You gave us an example of Sabbath rest for our good—spiritually and physically. May we faithfully set aside Your day for worship and rest. Amen.

Evening

To Grow or Not to Grow?

In this you greatly rejoice, even though now for a little while,
if necessary, you have been distressed by various trials, so that the proof of your faith,
being more precious than gold which is perishable, even though tested by fire,
may be found to result in praise and glory and honor at the revelation of Jesus Christ.
1 Peter 1:6–7 NASB

You're not alone in the hard times. Trust Him. He knows what He's doing.

God, thank You for difficulties and hard situations. I know that You're using them to help me grow. I really want to learn.

MORNING

Tears

Jesus wept.
JOHN 11:35 NIV

Jesus' tears demonstrate God's empathy as we go through the grieving process. God cares deeply about our situation. He desires to gather us in His arms. He understands the sorrow and turmoil we feel when we experience serious heartache.

Loving Lord, You know my tears. You value each of my tears so much that You gather them in Your bottle and write them in Your book. Thank You for understanding me.

EVENING

He Loves Me Anyway

Jesus replied, "Anyone who loves me will obey my teaching. My Father will love them, and we will come to them and make our home with them."
JOHN 14:23 NIV

You will always try your best to obey God's commandments, which is just what He wants you to do. But if you ever fail, He will love you anyway. And He'll gently guide you back to His embrace. Oh how He loves you!

God, thank You for loving me. No matter what, Your love is all-forgiving and Your Word is unfailing. Amen.

MORNING

The Days of Your Youth

Remember also your Creator in the days of your youth, before the evil days come and the years draw near when you will say, "I have no delight in them."
ECCLESIASTES 12:1 NASB

Have you forgotten the God of your youth? Have His principles been compromised away by the pressures of a world that teaches that the Ten Commandments are optional? With the Lord's help, it's not too late to turn it all around.

*Lord, if I look back and see a trail of regret,
please give me the courage to change the view.*

EVENING

Who Knows You Best?

"And he pays even greater attention to you, down to the last detail—even numbering the hairs on your head! So don't be intimidated by all this bully talk. You're worth more than a million canaries."
LUKE 12:7 MSG

God made you—He even knew you before you were born! And when the unexpected happens, always remember that the same God who knows you so well is also going to take care of you. You are His child, and He will see you through everything that comes your way.

*Dear God, please help me to always remember that You
know everything that happens to me—good or bad.*

MORNING

For His Own Good

And we know that all things work together for good to them that love God, to them who are the called according to his purpose.
ROMANS 8:28 KJV

Sometimes life's circumstances cause us to cry out, "Why, Lord? Why?" And God's response is always the same: so that His good work might be displayed in our lives.

Father, help me to trust You more. Help me to see Your hand at work and to let go of my desire for control. May Your glory be displayed in my life for all to see.

EVENING

On His Mind

What is man that You are mindful of him,
and the son of man that You visit him?
PSALM 8:4 NKJV

Do you think about God? Today, let your thoughts be centered on the One who loves you most. Let your words reveal your thoughts as you talk to other people about Him. Those thoughts and words reveal the true condition of your heart.

Dear God, please help me to control my thoughts today and let them be about You. Help me remember to speak truth to others and to keep my heart turned toward You. Amen.

DAY
150

MORNING

Present Help

For I, the LORD your God, hold your right hand; it is I who say to you, "Fear not, I am the one who helps you."
ISAIAH 41:13 ESV

He is with you in your most anxious moments and in your darkest hours. With the clasp of His hand comes courage for any situation. He tells you not to fear, for He is your ever-present help in times of trouble.

Almighty God, I am grateful that You hold my hand. Help me to remember I am never alone. Grant me the courage that comes from knowing You as my helper.

EVENING

Forgiveness

But God showed his great love for us by sending Christ to die for us while we were still sinners.
ROMANS 5:8 NLT

Think about the grace that God pours out on you as He forgives your sins. Do you show grace to other people when they make mistakes? One way that others can see God in you is through forgiveness. Choose to forgive today!

God, thank You for Your forgiveness.
Help me to be forgiving. Amen.

MORNING

Eye of the Beholder

So God created human beings in his own image. In the image of God he created them; male and female he created them.
GENESIS 1:27 NLT

When it comes to self-image, let's not view our own perceived flaws as negatives. Let's see ourselves through God's eyes, remembering that His creation is always good.

Dear Lord, when I look in the mirror, remind me that I was created in Your image and that, although I may not always see myself as beautiful, You think I look very good.

EVENING

Envy

The boundary lines have fallen for me in pleasant places; surely I have a delightful inheritance.
PSALM 16:6 NIV

The person who is envious doesn't believe that God is giving her exactly what she needs. If we knew He was giving us the very best for us, then we would never be envious.

Lord, please help me to trust You so that I am never envious. Help me to be happy for those around me when they are blessed. Thank You for giving each of us just what we need. Amen.

DAY
152

Morning

Jesus, the Good Shepherd

"He who enters by the door is a shepherd of the sheep.
To him the doorkeeper opens, and the sheep hear his voice,
and he calls his own sheep by name and leads them out."
John 10:2–3 NASB

God calls us by name, just as the shepherd has pet names for his sheep. Someday, when the King of kings, our Good Shepherd, calls us home to heaven, we'll hear the name He calls us.

Lord, guide me to safe pastures today. Never leave me.

Evening

Live to Give!

"Love your neighbor as yourself."
Leviticus 19:18 NIV

The Bible tells us that love is not selfish or self-seeking, but that's one of those verses that is much easier to read than live. Ask God to help you put others' needs above your own. Look for ways to be a better friend. Live the love!

God, please help me to live to give, and help me
to love my friends the way You love me. Amen.

MORNING

God's Mirror

Charm is deceptive, and beauty does not last;
but a woman who fears the LORD will be greatly praised.
PROVERBS 31:30 NLT

Today, gaze into the mirror of scripture. Allow your true beauty to be that inner beauty of soul—a reflection of Christ—that never fades.

Father, thank You for the beauty that You reflect from my soul.
Help me to place less importance on my outward appearance and more value
on the inner qualities that You are developing in me.

EVENING

Integrity and Truth

"And you will know the truth, and the truth will set you free."
JOHN 8:32 NLT

Mark Twain said, "Always tell the truth. That way, you don't have to remember what you said." When you make daily choices that honor God, such as being honest and trustworthy, you don't ever have to worry about being caught in a lie. And that's a freeing feeling!

Jesus, I know You are always looking,
and I want to honor You with my life.

Morning

Perfect Guidance

*May the Lord direct your hearts into the love
of God and into the steadfastness of Christ.*
2 Thessalonians 3:5 NASB

Praise be to God for giving us His Spirit, who resides in us so that we need never lose our direction as we navigate our way through life.

*Thank You, Jesus, for sending Your Holy Spirit
to lead me in the right direction. Amen.*

Evening

What to Wear

*"And why do you worry about clothes? See how the flowers
of the field grow. They do not labor or spin. Yet I tell you that not
even Solomon in all his splendor was dressed like one of these."*
Matthew 6:28–29 NIV

God may not always give us every single thing we want. But He knows what we need, and He will provide it, if we just ask Him and trust Him with the results.

*Dear Father, thank You for providing me with everything I need.
Help me to appreciate the things You provide.*

MORNING

When God Redecorates

God is the builder of everything.
HEBREWS 3:4 NIV

If we let Him, He'll replace the temporary supports we rely on—health, independence, ability, you name it—with eternal spiritual supports like faith, surrender, and prayer. Those supports enable us to live a life of true freedom, one abounding with spiritual blessing.

Lord, I am tempted to cling to the supports I've erected.
When my life crashes, I'm tempted to despair. Please help me
to be still and place my trust in You, the great builder of all lives.

EVENING

Heavenly Language

Sound speech, that cannot be condemned.
TITUS 2:8 KJV

While you can't entirely avoid hearing the world's language, you can limit what goes into your ears. Most of all, keep tight control of your own thoughts and speech. Remember that you represent God. . .and He is always listening!

Dear Father, I know that You don't want me to use bad language.
Help me always to keep my speech pure so that I can glorify You. Amen.

DAY
156

Morning

Isaiah, a Major Prophet

Listen, O heavens, and hear, O earth; for the LORD speaks, "Sons I have reared and brought up, but they have revolted against Me. . . . My people do not understand."
ISAIAH 1:2–3 NASB

Reading Isaiah provides a necessary heart check. Like Israel, if we fail to turn from our defiant ways, we must ask, "Where will you be stricken again, as you continue in your rebellion?" (Isaiah 1:5 NASB).

Lord, open my mind to receive Your truth. And keep me from confusion, that I might know You as both Messiah and Lord.

Evening

Drop Anchor!

This hope we have as an anchor of the soul, a hope both sure and steadfast.
HEBREWS 6:19 NASB

Just as the anchor on a boat holds it steady. God is the anchor of your soul, and He's offering you *His* hope, which is true and everlasting. Allow Him to anchor you. Seek Him in everything you do, and He will guide you toward an even greater future.

Lord, sometimes I feel so lost. The choices and decisions I have to make overwhelm me, and I'm not sure which way to go. Please be my anchor.

Morning

Sowing the Wind

They sow the wind and they reap the whirlwind.
Hosea 8:7 NASB

Take a deep breath. Take a long walk. Depart from the rat race. Relax in God's arms. Keep your eyes on Christ instead of worldly goods, and you will reap not the earthly whirlwind but heavenly treasure.

God, keep my eyes on the right prize—Your Son, Jesus Christ. Help me to slow down, walk in Your will, and become a blessing in this world, always looking toward the next. Amen.

Evening

Streets of Gold, Really?

The twelve gates were twelve pearls; each gate was made from a single pearl. The street of the city was of pure gold, transparent as glass.
Revelation 21:21 GNT

Think of how much God loved us—enough to make a beautiful home for us to live forever. Everyone wants to know they will have an eternal home. And who wouldn't want to dwell in the most beautiful place we could possibly imagine?

Heavenly Father, I'm so grateful that You accept me as Your child and that I get to spend eternity with You. Amen.

Morning

Rachel's Saddlebags

Rachel had taken the household gods and put them in a camel's saddlebag and was sitting on them. Laban searched through the whole tent, but did not find them.
Genesis 31:34 GNT

From our twenty-first-century vantage point, it's easy to wag a finger at Rachel. But in Rachel's day, those little idols were pervasive, part of the culture. She didn't dismiss Jacob's God—she just added to Him and she allowed idols to replace God's primary position in her life.

Let's take care to keep God exactly where He belongs, in first place.

Lord, clean my house! Open my eyes to the worthless idols in my life. Teach me to desire only You.

Evening

God Is Always with Me

I will be with you always, even until the end of the world.
Matthew 28:20 CEV

Since God is our constant companion, it would work best for us to give Him the leader position and follow where He leads. He will never try to get away or "lose" us. He wants us to be following closely, maintaining a close relationship with Him.

Dear Jesus, You have promised to always be with me. No one else shows that kind of devotion. Thank You for loving me so much that You want to be with me! Amen.

Morning

What Are Your Gifts?

There are different kinds of gifts, but the same Spirit distributes them. There are different kinds of service, but the same Lord.
1 Corinthians 12:4–5 niv

Today, thank the Lord for entrusting you with spiritual gifts. If you're struggling to know where you fit, ask Him to give you opportunities to minister in different areas until you find just the right spot.

Lord, thank You for pouring out Your Spirit on me, and thank You for the gifts You've placed within me.

Evening

Doing the Impossible

A hard worker has plenty of food, but a person who chases fantasies has no sense. . . . Work hard and become a leader; be lazy and become a slave.
Proverbs 12:11, 24 nlt

Whatever you do, work at it with all your heart. Other people are looking up to you. So don't cut corners. Don't be lazy. Work hard, and soon you'll be doing the impossible!

God, I've never really thought of myself as a leader, but I guess I am! Help me to be a better one and a hard worker for those who look up to me.

DAY
160

MORNING

Life Preservers

My comfort in my suffering is this:
Your promise preserves my life.
PSALM 119:50 NIV

In the difficulties of life, God is our life preserver. When we are battered by the waves of trouble, we can expect God to understand and to comfort us in our distress. His Word, like a buoyant life preserver, holds us up in the bad times.

Preserving God, I cling to You as my life preserver. Keep my head above the turbulent water of caregiving so I don't drown. Bring me safely to the shore.

EVENING

You Promised!

"God is not a man, that He should lie."
NUMBERS 23:19 NKJV

The Bible is full of promises that He's kept and *still keeps* consistently today. His track record is worthy and full of integrity. At times we may start to believe He is not going to keep His promises, at least where we are concerned. But chances are, we don't realize He's simply not going to keep a promise in the way we expect Him to.

God, help me to be patient as I wait on You. I know I need to trust Your promises will happen in Your way. Amen.

Morning

An Invitation to Dine

"The kingdom of heaven may be compared to
a king who gave a wedding feast for his son."
Matthew 22:2 NASB

When God sent His Son to earth, He invited all men and women to a wedding feast. Those who accept the invitation become part of the Church. And the Church is the bride of Christ. But there are many who have offered feeble excuses for their lack of faith.

Lord, You've invited me to dine with You.
Let me graciously accept my "wedding clothes."

Evening

Want to Hang Out with Me?

You are all around me, behind me and
in front of me. You hold me in your hand.
Psalm 139:5 NIrV

Are you lonely today? Need someone to hang out with? Why not hang out with the King of kings and Lord of lords? He will wipe away your loneliness and remind you that you are loved. Best of all, He's already there, right beside you, waiting for you to say, "Hey, let's hang out together!"

God, I'm glad You're not too busy to hang out with me.

DAY
162

Morning

A Shadow of the Past

"Only Rahab the prostitute and all who are with her in her house shall be spared, because she hid the spies we sent."
Joshua 6:17 TNIV

We all have to deal with a past. All of us! Disappointments, poor choices, dysfunctional families, parents who failed us, husbands who harmed us. God is able to bring good from even those years that were painful. By the grace and power of God we can make choices in the present that can affect our future.

Holy Spirit, You are always at work.
Don't ever stop! Show me a new way, Lord.

Evening

Watch Your Mouth

From the fruit of their lips people enjoy good things. . . .
Those who guard their lips preserve their lives.
Proverbs 13:2–3 NIV

What are the right things? Whatever God's Word says. No matter what the situation, always make sure you find out what God's Word says about it. Then *you* say what *God* says. "I can do all things through Christ!" "The Lord cares for me because I trust Him." "By His stripes I am healed."

Dear God, help me to remember the power of my words.
Teach me to use them well. Amen.

Morning

Toss Those Boxing Gloves!

Avoiding a fight is a mark of honor; only fools insist on quarreling.
Proverbs 20:3 NLT

You have to follow the Golden Rule—doing unto others as you would have them do unto you. And you have to love others as you would love yourself.

Lord, I ask You today to be at the center of my friendships, especially the difficult ones. Show me what to say and what not to say to avoid strife. Give me Your heart toward my friends.

Evening

Eternal Perspective

Work willingly at whatever you do, as though you were working for the Lord rather than for people.
Colossians 3:23 NLT

An eternal perspective. What in the world does that mean? That is the idea behind this verse summed up into two, easy-to-remember words. Having an "eternal perspective" means that you realize all the work you do right now—your job, your chores at home, how you treat others—that all means something to God! And not just for right now! It means something for all eternity.

God, thanks for watching over me and guiding me. Help me to do my work remembering that it is ultimately for You.

DAY
164

Morning

Do We Need to Do It All?

I have glorified thee on the earth: I have finished the work which thou gavest me to do.
John 17:4 kjv

Simply because we can do all things through Christ doesn't mean He is calling us to do everything. If we would be like Jesus, we will do only the work the Father gives us, not all the work we can do.

Dear Father, give me eyes to see where You are working so that I may work with You. Help me rebuff the world's temporal demands so that I can focus on heavenly duties that bring eternal rewards. Amen.

Evening

God's Design

I praise you because I am fearfully and wonderfully made; your works are wonderful, I know that full well.
Psalm 139:14 niv

God made your body, and He designed your face exactly how He wanted it. He knew you before anyone else ever even saw you. He thinks you're perfect. It doesn't matter how much you weigh, how tall you are, or the kinds of clothes you wear. You are His beloved. And what's best is He knows your heart and loves you still.

Dear God, please help me to love myself so I can be a reflection of You to those around me. Amen.

MORNING

In God We Trust

"For forty years I led you through the wilderness, yet your clothes and sandals did not wear out. . .so you would know that he is the LORD your God."
DEUTERONOMY 29:5–6 NLT

When the children of Israel suffered under their Egyptian oppressors, God freed them with signs and wonders. Then for forty years they wandered in the desert, and each day they had just enough food and water to sustain them. God will do the same for us. Put your trust in Him.

*Lord, thank You that You promise to take care of us.
Help us not to put too much trust in men or agencies.*

EVENING

My Guide

*So I say, let the Holy Spirit guide your lives.
Then you won't be doing what your sinful nature craves.*
GALATIANS 5:16 NLT

We all mess up. And without someone to guide us, we would be lost forever. Jesus says, "I am the way and the truth and the life. No one comes to the Father except through me" (John 14:6 NIV).

Dear Jesus, thank You for loving me so much that You gave up Your life to save me. Thank You for a fresh start. Thank You for being my guide.

DAY
166

Morning

Jesus Raises Lazarus

Now a certain man was sick, Lazarus of Bethany. . . . The sisters sent word to [Jesus], saying, "Lord, behold, he whom You love is sick."
John 11:1, 3 NASB

When we hear that a good friend is critically ill, we run to his side. Why then does Jesus tarry? "But when Jesus heard this, He said, 'This sickness is not to end in death, but for the glory of God, so that the Son of God may be glorified by it' " (John 11:4 NASB).

Lord, strengthen my faith so that when tragedy strikes,
I know that You are the Resurrection and the Life.

Evening

He Knows You—and Loves You

You have searched me, Lord, and you know me. You know when I sit and when I rise; you perceive my thoughts from afar. You discern my going out and my lying down; you are familiar with all my ways. Before a word is on my tongue you, Lord, know it completely.
Psalm 139:1–4 NIV

God knows the sins you have already committed and the sins of your future. And He loves you. He knows your heart. His arms will surround you in love and protection forever.

God, thank You for letting me be me. Amen.

MORNING

Daughter of the King

You are all children of God through faith.
GALATIANS 3:26 NIV

If you have a child of your own, consider the unconditional love you feel for him or her. As intense as that love is, because you are human, you are limited in your ability to love. In contrast, God loves us in a way we will not fully understand until we reach heaven.

Thank You, Father, for adopting me through Christ as Your daughter. Teach me to live as a reflection of my Father's love. Amen.

EVENING

Does God Really Care?

We are afflicted in every way, but not crushed; perplexed, but not despairing; persecuted, but not forsaken; struck down, but not destroyed; always carrying about in the body the dying of Jesus, so that the life of Jesus also may be manifested in our body.
2 CORINTHIANS 4:8–10 NASB

You're so precious in the sight of God. Every move you make, every breath you take, every thought you think. . .He knows it all.

Father, thank You for taking care of me. I'm in total awe that You care so much about me. Thank You. In Jesus' name I pray. Amen.

DAY
168

Morning

I've Fallen and I Can't Get Up

The godly may trip seven times, but they will get up again.
Proverbs 24:16 NLT

However many times we fall, our heavenly Father never gives up on us. He never leaves us to ourselves, to stagger to our feet alone. God is always present with us, encouraging us to keep trying—regardless of past failures—picking us up, dusting us off, and setting us on our way again.

Heavenly Father, it's such a comfort to know You will never leave me or forsake me.

Evening

Read the Instructions

All Scripture is inspired by God and is useful to teach us what is true and to make us realize what is wrong in our lives.
2 Timothy 3:16 NLT

The Bible is God's instruction book for life. If you jump into life without reading scripture, you won't know God's will or His ways. You may start out on a wrong path. You won't receive the warnings that His Word contains for your good.

Thank You, Lord, for giving me instructions for life. Create in me a love for scripture, I pray. Amen.

Morning

Expect Trouble

These things I have spoken unto you, that in me ye might have peace. In the world ye shall have tribulation: but be of good cheer; I have overcome the world.
John 16:33 KJV

Expect trouble, but refuse to let it defeat you. Trials strengthen our faith and our character. No one gets excited about a trial, yet we can be assured that God is still in control even when trouble comes our way.

Lord Jesus, be my strength as I face trouble in this life.
Walk with me. Hold my hand.

Evening

Obey? No Way!

For God is working in you, giving you the desire and the power to do what pleases him.
Philippians 2:13 NLT

Obedience is a tough one. But here's the good news. If you're a Christian, God is constantly working on your heart so that you'll want to obey Him. He will never give up on you. He doesn't dwell on your disobedience. Instead, He sees you through eyes of love. Ask Him to help you, and remember today is a great day to obey!

God, help me to become more obedient. Amen.

DAY 170

Morning

A Counselor for the Troubled

"In My Father's house are many dwelling places."
John 14:2 NASB

Jesus Christ has promised to prepare a place for us in heaven. Does it get any better than that? The only problem is that we have to wait down here until He's got our mansion ready for us. There are days when it's so hard to stay tied to earth, especially with the realization that a perfect place exists.

Lord, thank You for the Holy Spirit, who brings us peace and comfort until we can be united with You in heaven.

Evening

God Loves Me

God's love, though, is ever and always, eternally present to all who fear him, making everything right for them and their children.
Psalm 103:17 MSG

God doesn't ever stop loving because we are unlovable. In fact, His love is something we can count on and always trust to be there. If we do wrong, all we need to do is ask His forgiveness, and He will give it to us because He loves us. God will help us do better and make things right again for us if we turn to Him.

Dear God, thank You for loving me always.

MORNING

The Waiting Game

LORD, I wait for you; you will answer, Lord my God.
PSALM 38:15 NIV

God's timing is certainly not ours. But as we wait on Him, we can be confident that He is never too early and never too late. Wait patiently and with confidence. God *will* come through.

Heavenly Father, when the waiting seems unbearable, remind me that Your timing is always perfect. Amen.

EVENING

I'm Forgiven

As for our transgressions, You forgive them.
PSALM 65:3 NASB

There will be days when you stand strong to temptation, and there will be days when you fail. But praise God—He is there, loving you, wanting to pick you up and dust you off. Confess your mistakes to Him, and bask in His amazing grace. You are forgiven!

Heavenly Father, please help me to stand strong today in the face of temptation and help me to share Your forgiveness with someone else today. Amen.

MORNING

Charm Bracelet

But the fruit of the Spirit is love, joy, peace, patience, kindness, goodness, faithfulness, gentleness, self-control; against such things there is no law.
GALATIANS 5:22–23 NASB

Ask your Father which areas in your Christian walk need the most growth. Do you need to develop those traits more strongly before you feel comfortable donning your bracelet?

Lord, please show me which milestones of Christian living I need to focus on in order to have the full markings of the Holy Spirit in my life. Please help me to grow into the Christian woman You call me to be. Amen.

EVENING

You Have a History

"Fear not, for I am with you; be not dismayed,
for I am your God. I will strengthen you, yes, I will help you,
I will uphold you with My righteous right hand."
ISAIAH 41:10 NKJV

When life gets tough, it pays to remember our history with the heavenly Father. By remembering the ways He protected and sent support, we can gain the courage to move through to the next great season in our lives—and we can feel grateful for what we have *right now*.

God, thank You for all You do for me—
even if life does get a little tough at times. Amen.

Morning

Attitude Is Everything

A cheerful disposition is good for your health;
gloom and doom leave you bone-tired.
Proverbs 17:22 msg

Sometimes we have to fake it till we feel it. Experiment with this strategy today. Put a smile on your face when you feel discouraged over a setback or frustrated about an inconvenience. A cheerful heart is good medicine.

Father, thank You for this day You have given me.
Create in me a happy heart. Amen.

Evening

Seeing Beauty with the Eyes of the Heart

I pray that the eyes of your heart may be enlightened.
Ephesians 1:18 niv

In the Bible, it says that we have "eyes of the heart." Eyes of the heart help us to see what God sees, and they help us to love what He loves. Sometimes others may not have God's eyes to see the beauty in us. This doesn't mean you aren't beautiful.

Jesus, thank You that You have perfect vision and that You always see my beauty.
Because You made me, I am always beautiful to You. I love You, Lord. Amen.

MORNING

Aiding the Enemy

And she said unto her mistress, "Would God my lord were with the prophet that is in Samaria! for he would recover him of his leprosy."
2 KINGS 5:3 KJV

The Lord did not forget the young girl, alone in a difficult world. And the lessons her parents had taught her made a difference not only in her life, but also in the lives of unbelievers around her.

Father, I do not know the paths I will take, whether happy or sad. But please let the truths You have taught me glorify You.

EVENING

Rainbows and Promises

He will keep his agreement forever;
he will keep his promises always.
PSALM 105:8 NCV

When we become God's children, He promises to love us, protect us, guide us, and then take us to heaven to live with Him forever when our time on earth is done. What amazing promises!

Dear Father, I know that You will be faithful to keep Your word. Help me to faithfully keep the promises I make, too. In Jesus' name, amen.

MORNING

An Intimate Conversation

"This is eternal life, that they may know You, the only true God, and Jesus Christ whom You have sent. I glorified You on the earth, having accomplished the work which You have given Me to do."
JOHN 17:3–4 NASB

Have you ever unwittingly overheard an intimate conversation? Well, that's exactly what this chapter of John is like. We are privileged to overhear Jesus as He speaks to the Father. Christ was with the Father before the world was. That makes Him not only eternal but equal with the Father.

Lord Jesus Christ, I acknowledge You as God and Savior.

EVENING

What's So Scary?

"I am leaving you with a gift—peace of mind and heart. And the peace I give is a gift the world cannot give. So don't be troubled or afraid."
JOHN 14:27 NLT

It isn't part of God's plan for you to be stopped in your tracks because you're feeling afraid and alone. He will help you fight the battle; all you need to do is ask for His protection and peace. Then clear your mind, and get to work on becoming the woman He wants you to be.

Dear Lord, thank You that You are always with me and helping me be who I was meant to be. Amen.

DAY
176

MORNING

Faithful One

Let us hold unswervingly to the hope we profess,
for he who promised is faithful.
HEBREWS 10:23 NIV

By holding tightly to the hope we have, we can benefit those around us who are struggling to find hope of their own. We can spur another hurting woman on to love and goodness and, in so doing, help ourselves better understand the God in whom our hope lies.

Dear Jesus, I know You are faithful—but I often forget that. Show me how to live every minute today to spur others toward Your love tomorrow.

EVENING

Hopeful

May the God of hope fill you with all joy and peace as you trust in him,
so that you may overflow with hope by the power of the Holy Spirit.
ROMANS 15:13 NIV

With God, we always have hope for a better future! We can know, without any doubt, that things will get better for us. God loves us, and He has good things in store for us. And we can do those things because of that one little word: *hope.*

Dear Father, thank You for giving me hope.
When things seem hopeless, help me to trust in Your love for me.

Morning

God Has Left the Building

And the curtain of the temple was torn in two.
Luke 23:45 NIV

God is an unchanging God who seeks relationship with us just as He did throughout biblical history. But we no longer have to walk the streets of Jerusalem to find God's Spirit. He comes to us and finds us just where we are.

Holy God, I invite You to make Your temple within me.
I pledge that all I do will show honor to You and give You praise.

Evening

Shine or Grumble?

Do all things without grumbling or disputing, that you may be blameless and innocent, children of God without blemish in the midst of a crooked and twisted generation, among whom you shine as lights in the world, holding fast to the word of life.
Philippians 2:14–16 ESV

God's Word tells us that "His divine power has given us everything we need for a godly life through our knowledge of him who called us by his own glory and goodness" (2 Peter 1:3 NIV).

God, there are lots of times I want to grumble and complain,
but please help me to focus on my blessings and not my problems.

DAY 178

MORNING

Slipped Moorings

But Jonah ran away from the LORD. . . . He went down to Joppa, where he found a ship bound for that port. After paying the fare, he went aboard and sailed for Tarshish to flee from the LORD.
JONAH 1:3 NIV

You can walk away from God, but you can't escape Him. Even if you did, you would find yourself in a very lonely spot. A huge piece of your heart, God's piece, would be missing.

Turn my heart always to You, Lord. I never want to leave You. Amen.

EVENING

Count on It!

Through His shining-greatness and perfect life, He has given us promises. These promises are of great worth and no amount of money can buy them.
2 PETER 1:4 NLV

See, with God, what He says is what He will do. In other words, He always keeps His promises! If you want to know more, read your Bible. It's loaded with great promises just for you!

Dear Lord, thanks for giving me Your Word. Amen.

Morning

Well of Salvation

With joy you will draw water from the wells of salvation.
Isaiah 12:3 esv

Our salvation is a well. In it is not only our eternal life, but also our abundant life while we live on earth. Christ is the Living Water, continually refreshing and nourishing us, giving life to our bodies and souls. He is strength when we are weak, wisdom when we are foolish, hope when we are despondent, and life when we are dying.

Lord, thank You for saving me. Thank You for being the Living Water, my continual source of peace, comfort, strength, and joy.

Evening

Precious, Uncountable Thoughts

How precious are your thoughts about me, O God.
They cannot be numbered!
Psalm 139:17 nlt

You are precious to your Creator. There is nothing He does not know about you, yet despite any flaws, He wants you. He has big plans for you. And He loves you more than you can ever imagine!

Dear heavenly Father, thank You
for creating me and for Your love for me.

DAY 180

Morning

Question the Witnesses

"Why do you question Me? Question those who have heard what I spoke to them; they know what I said."
John 18:21 NASB

Jesus Christ didn't come for a few souls; He presented the Gospel message openly for all to hear. Teaching in the Jewish temple, which was frequented not only by those who sought knowledge but also those in search of an explanation of the truth, Jesus provided both.

Lord, break down my walls of stubbornness, which prevent me from hearing, seeing, and rallying to Your message.

Evening

God Has a Plan

"For I know the plans I have for you," declares the Lord*, "plans to prosper you and not to harm you, plans to give you hope and a future."*
Jeremiah 29:11 NIV

Do things ever seem to go wrong and just keep going wrong for you? Life's not always easy, but remember that God has good plans for you. He will see you through the tough times and get you past any illness and disappointments. He knows the plans for your future, even if you don't.

Dear God, help me to remember that You do have a plan, even if I don't know what it is right now. Amen.

MORNING

Sabbath Queen

"Observe the Sabbath day, to keep it holy."
EXODUS 20:8 MSG

Lauren F. Winner, a messianic Jew and author of *Mudhouse Sabbath*, writes, "We spoke of the day as *Shabbat haMalka*, the Sabbath Queen, and we sang hymns of praise on Friday night that welcomed the Sabbath as a bride."

Welcome the Sabbath Queen to your home this week.

Lord, help me practice a rhythm of rest and restoration, weekly welcoming the Sabbath, restoring order and worship to my weary soul. Amen.

EVENING

Heirs for All Eternity

If you belong to Christ, then you are Abraham's descendants, heirs according to promise.
GALATIANS 3:29 NASB

We're not just heirs, we're daughters of God through our faith; we've "received adoption" (Galatians 4:4–6). He's preparing a place for you in heaven and will fulfill His covenant to you. He will *never* abandon you (2 Corinthians 4:8–18). God always keeps His promises, and He will never leave you to wander in this dark world alone.

Lord, thank You so much for making me an heir through my faith in Your Son, Jesus.

DAY
182

Morning

Shake It Off

Then [Paul simply] shook off the small creature
into the fire and suffered no evil effects.
Acts 28:5 amp

Don't allow your mistakes to so worry or condemn you that you can't be helpful to others around you. The poison of stress and worry will harm us if we allow it to penetrate our hearts and minds. Follow Paul's example: shake it off.

Dear Lord, thank You for cleansing me of my sins. I will not worry or feel condemned any longer. Thank You, Lord, for helping me to shake things off and suffer no evil effects.

Evening

Choosing Your Friends

The righteous choose their friends carefully,
but the way of the wicked leads them astray.
Proverbs 12:26 niv

It's good to be kind and loving to everyone, but it's so important that your closest companions love Jesus. You won't seek to cause each other to fall down, but instead you can spot one another on the balance beam of life.

Lord, I want to thank You for Christian friends who encourage me to walk in Your ways. Amen.

MORNING

You Are What You Cling To

Hate what is evil; cling to what is good.
ROMANS 12:9 NIV

Beware of your temptations. Know your areas of vulnerability and avoid them. Instead, draw close to the Lord. Allow Him to satisfy your deepest longings. When we cling to good, evil loses its grip.

Dear Lord, help me avoid temptation. May I draw close to You so I can cling to good and avoid evil in my life. Amen.

EVENING

All Things Fabulous

And my God will meet all your needs according to the riches of his glory in Christ Jesus.
PHILIPPIANS 4:19 NIV

God cares more about you than to just give you everything you want. God gives you everything you need, and that promise won't ever fade or tarnish or be forgotten at the bottom of a drawer!

Lord, thank You for giving me everything I need. And forgive me that sometimes when I'm so busy asking You for more, I forget to thank You for what I already have. Amen.

DAY 184

Morning

Quick and Slow

My dear brothers and sisters, take note of this: Everyone should be quick to listen, slow to speak and slow to become angry, because human anger does not produce the righteousness that God desires.
JAMES 1:19–20 NIV

Practice being quick and slow today—quick to listen, slow to speak, slow to become angry.

God, grant me the patience, wisdom, and grace I need to be a good listener. Remind me also, Father, to use my words today to lift others up rather than to tear them down. Amen.

Evening

You Call. . .He Answers

I sought the LORD, and he answered me;
he delivered me from all my fears.
PSALM 34:4 NIV

God always answers, too, even though it may not seem like it. Because God is more interested in your character than your comfort, the answer may not be the one you were hoping for. Sometimes the answer is no. Sometimes the answer is "wait." And sometimes the answer is yes, but you don't recognize it because it doesn't look the way you thought it would.

Dear God, thank You for being a God of answers. Amen.

MORNING

Dependence Day

"Then the glory of the LORD will be revealed, and all flesh will see it together; for the mouth of the LORD has spoken."
ISAIAH 40:5 NASB

Jesus is the First and the Last. Christ clarifies this further in Revelation 1:8 (NASB): " 'I am the Alpha and the Omega,' says the Lord God, 'who is and who was and who is to come, the Almighty.' "

Lord Jesus, I rejoice in the words from Isaiah 53:4–6, that You came to be my Redeemer. Hallelujah! Amen!

EVENING

See You Later

Precious in the sight of the LORD is the death of his saints.
PSALM 116:15 KJV

Death is a part of life that always takes you by surprise. Life is truly a gift, and when someone we love dies, it leaves a painful hole in your life. But remember that you will see your loved ones again.

Lord, thank You for taking the sting from death. Comfort me with this knowledge when I must bid farewell to my loved ones, and help me keep heaven in view. Amen.

DAY
186

Morning

The Heart Test

You have tested my heart; You have visited me in the night; You have tried me and have found nothing; I have purposed that my mouth shall not transgress.
Psalm 17:3 NKJV

Let God do the work He wants to do in you—purging, purifying, and penetrating. Listen to His *"This is a test"* whisper; then stand firm. Don't yield to the temptation to give up or to say it's not worth it.

Lord, sometimes I feel like my heart is being tested by circumstances, relationships, or even by You. Help me to stand strong in what I know to be true.

Evening

Standing on the Promises

My eyes stay open through the watches of the night, that I may meditate on your promises.
Psalm 119:148 NIV

The rainbow—a vibrant burst of color: red, orange, yellow, green, blue, indigo, and violet. A beautiful reminder of God's unfailing promises and amazing love for you!

God, thank You for Your peace, rest, and love. Your promises are within my soul. I am standing on Your promises! Amen.

Morning

Board God's Boat

"Come with me by yourselves to a quiet place and get some rest."
Mark 6:31 niv

Often we allow the hectic pace of daily life to drain us physically and spiritually, and in the process, we deny ourselves time alone to pray and read God's Word. Meanwhile, God patiently waits.

So perhaps it's time to board God's boat to a quieter place and not jump ship!

Heavenly Father, in my hectic life I've neglected time apart with You. Help me to board Your boat and stay afloat through spending time in Your Word and in prayer. Amen.

Evening

Life Is Hard, but God Is Good

For just as the sufferings of Christ are ours in abundance, so also our comfort is abundant through Christ.
2 Corinthians 1:5 nasb

When you're in the middle of a trial, remind yourself to turn to your heavenly Father. His comfort is the only comfort you'll ever need, and it is abundant. There's plenty of it for every day of your life.

God, I need Your comfort. Help me to smile through the trials and keep my focus on You. Amen.

DAY
188

Morning

Ideal Place

For consider your calling, brethren, that there were not many wise according to the flesh, not many mighty, not many noble; but God has chosen the foolish things of the world.
1 Corinthians 1:26–27 NASB

God delights in using His people—right in the middle of all that appears crazy and wrong and hopeless. He wants our cheerful, obedient service right in the midst of—even in spite of—our difficult circumstances.

Father, help me see that there is no "ideal" place or circumstance to serve You.

Evening

Fight the Urge to Fight!

Do not repay anyone evil for evil.
Be careful to do what is right
in the eyes of everyone.
Romans 12:17 NIV

Don't let strife camp out in your life. Instead, fight the urge to fight! You'll be so glad you did.

God, help me to walk in love, not strife. Help me to be a peacemaker in all my relationships. I love You, Amen.

Morning

Fear of the Lord

The fear of the Lord *leads to life;*
then one rests content, untouched by trouble.
Proverbs 19:23 niv

To fear the Lord is to respect Him and acknowledge that His ways are best for us. Our Abba Father, a gracious and loving God, is also a just and mighty God who is saddened, and even angered, by continuous, deliberate sin.

Lord, I respect You. Help me to acknowledge that You are God, You know best, and You have given me guidelines by which to live. Amen.

Evening

Can You Hear Me?

But when you ask him,
be sure that your faith is in God alone.
James 1:6 nlt

Hearing God's voice isn't always easy. A lot of noise fills up our lives. If you need an answer, make sure you find some alone time and practice listening for His instruction. Most of all, be patient. . .because His answer comes in His timing—not ours.

God, I need to hear Your voice today. I commit to finding a place where just You and I can hang out for a while. Amen.

DAY
190

Morning

Jonathan, Faithful to the End

Now the Philistines were fighting against Israel, and the men of
Israel fled from before the Philistines and fell slain on Mount Gilboa.
The Philistines overtook Saul and his sons; and the Philistines killed
Jonathan and Abinadab and Malchi-shua the sons of Saul.
1 Samuel 31:1–2 NASB

Who has faithfully stood beside you through life's triumphs and tragedies? For David this person was Jonathan.

Father, help me to be a faithful, loving, and unforgettable friend.

Evening

He Made Me

Your hands have made me and fashioned me;
give me understanding, that I may learn Your commandments.
Psalm 119:73 NKJV

In this world we live in, it is sometimes hard to grasp the fact that our God made us. That He made us each unique, and that He knows everything about us. He knows our weaknesses and our strengths; and He knows when we do wrong and when we do right. He knows everything that has happened and everything that will happen to us. And we owe Him everything.

Help me to know Your will, Father. Amen.

MORNING

Mountain-Moving Company

"If you have faith as small as a mustard seed, you can say to this mountain, 'Move from here to there,' and it will move. Nothing will be impossible for you."
MATTHEW 17:20 NIV

God can move mountains. He will show us the direction He wants us to take. He may move the mountain; or He may carry us over, around, or through it.

Lord God, You are the God of the impossible. We trust You to move the mountains of our lives and to move us through them. Amen.

EVENING

Temptation Nation

No temptation has overtaken you that is not common to man.
1 CORINTHIANS 10:13 ESV

Every morning, put on the full armor of God knowing that you are headed into battle. Remember, God is faithful; and He will always give you an escape! Be on the lookout!

God, help me to be strong in You today! Cover me with Your power, and protect me from the devil's plans. Help me do the right thing and always stand up for what I believe in. Amen.

DAY
192

Morning

Good Morning

Anyone who runs ahead and does not continue in the teaching of Christ does not have God; whoever continues in the teaching has both the Father and the Son.
2 John 1:9 NIV

Jesus gave us strong doctrines and good teaching to lead us into His truth. Faithful expositors cling to His Word from morning until night.

Keep me aware of Your truth, Lord.
I want to live on it, not on mush. Amen.

Evening

When Joy Is Hard

Let perseverance finish its work so that you
may be mature and complete, not lacking anything.
James 1:4 NIV

Next time things seem to be going all wrong, take a moment and thank God. Let's remind ourselves that God must be doing something pretty special. And let's smile, knowing God's plans for us are always good, even when they don't seem good at the time.

Dear Father, help me to be joyful even in the hard times. Thank You for caring about who I am tomorrow and not just about how I feel today.

MORNING

Still Waters

*"They will lie down on good grazing ground and feed in rich pasture. . . .
I will feed My flock and I will lead them to rest," declares the Lord God.*
EZEKIEL 34:14–15 NASB

God promises to lead us to lush, green pastures, while restoring our soul. Let's take Him up on the offer!

Heavenly Father, I need to learn to simply rest and relax. I see so much to do and have so much responsibility—so please enable me to lie down in the pastures You have provided.

EVENING

God's Love for Me

The person who has My commands and keeps them is the one who [really] loves Me; and whoever [really] loves Me will be loved by My Father, and I [too] will love him and will show (reveal, manifest) Myself to him. [I will let Myself be clearly seen by him and make Myself real to him.]
JOHN 14:21 AMP

But God loved us before we ever knew Him. He loved us when we knew Him but didn't love Him back. We hurt Him and offended Him, yet He kept on loving us.

Dear God, thank You for loving me when I'm not very lovable and for promising to always love me. In Jesus' name, amen.

DAY
194

MORNING

Keep Running

Let us run with perseverance the race marked out for us.
HEBREWS 12:1 NIV

Are you exhausted and overwhelmed? Remember that God is always watching, always encouraging.

Father, when the race is too much for me, give me strength for the journey. Thank You for the friends I have along the way. Help me to finish with confidence. Amen.

EVENING

The Fairy Tale

Instead, your beauty should consist of your true inner self, the ageless beauty of a gentle and quiet spirit, which is of the greatest value in God's sight.
1 PETER 3:4 GNT

What a boring world this would be if we all looked alike. Of course, every woman wants to be beautiful, but what kind of "beautiful" is the most important? Good looks come and go, but a kind heart and a love for God will take you further in life than anything on the outside possibly could.

Heavenly Father, thank You for creating me just the way I am.

Morning

Ezekiel's Call

While I was by the river Chebar among the exiles,
the heavens were opened and I saw visions of God.
Ezekiel 1:1 NASB

Ezekiel's visions parallel those of John recorded in the book of Revelation. These dreams show that no matter how bleak Israel's present situation might be, their future will be bright.

Lord, despite my own problems and challenges I can keep going forward as long as You show me a vision of hope. As I read the prophecies of Ezekiel, fill me with expectation!

Evening

Rejoice Always?

Rejoice always, pray without ceasing, in everything give thanks;
for this is the will of God in Christ Jesus for you.
1 Thessalonians 5:16–18 NKJV

Jesus knows there are times when your heart hurts. He understands that you don't always feel like jumping for joy. But what Jesus does want you to know is that He is always there. He calls you to trust Him to work good things from the bad in your life.

Father, I trust You to work all things together for good in my life. I thank You, even in the hard times. Amen.

DAY 196

Morning

Laying Down Your Life

Greater love hath no man than this,
that a man lay down his life for his friends.
John 15:13 KJV

Sacrifice, by its very definition, is the ability to place another's needs before your own—to continue pouring out, even when you're tapped out. Every instance you give of your time, energy, or resources to care for a loved one in need, you demonstrate your willingness to lay down your life. You're expressing the heart of God.

Dear Lord, please create a caregiver's heart within me—
a heart ready to give sacrificially no matter the cost.

Evening

He Is Always with Me, Part One

The Lord is my rock and my fortress and my deliverer, my God, my rock,
in whom I take refuge; my shield and the horn of my salvation, my stronghold.
Psalm 18:2 NASB

God is calling you, beautiful one (John 10:3)! Turn into His arms. Take His outstretched hand, and don't let go! When the devil "prowls around like a roaring lion" (1 Peter 5:8 NASB), keep your eyes on your glorious Lord. He's your Savior. And He's always here.

Lord, please help me to keep my eyes on You. In Jesus' name I pray. Amen.

Morning

A Child in Need

"For all those things My hand has made, and all those things exist," says the Lord. "But on this one will I look: on him who is poor and of a contrite spirit, and who trembles at My word."
Isaiah 66:2 NKJV

What needs do you have in your life today? Raise your hand in prayer to God. He'll take care of your needs and then some—blessing your life in ways you can't even imagine!

Father, thank You for caring about the needs of Your children. Help me to remember always to seek You first.

Evening

He Is Always with Me, Part Two

Do you not know that you are a temple of God and that the Spirit of God dwells in you?
1 Corinthians 3:16 NASB

God is our Father, and we're His children. He's here with us and in us. And just like a loving father, He guides and directs us through His Holy Spirit (John 14:16; 16:13; Romans 8:26).

Lord, please help me to keep my focus on You and never forget that You're always with me. In Jesus' holy name I pray. Amen.

Morning

Look Up, Not Around

But in all this comparing and grading
and competing, they quite miss the point.
2 Corinthians 10:12 msg

If we strive toward our goals in a way that causes other believers to stumble or violates the values God has set forth for us, then perhaps we should take a step back. After all, our final victory has little to do with what the world thinks about us.

Father God, Your standards are what I need to hold before me. Grant me the wisdom to keep Your values in mind as I aim for any higher goal. Amen.

Evening

Bees and God's Plan for Me

For we are God's handiwork, created in Christ Jesus to
do good works, which God prepared in advance for us to do.
Ephesians 2:10 niv

I once read that every three mouthfuls of food we eat are because there was some fuzzy bee somewhere doing his job. It makes sense that if God has a plan for the tiny bee, that He has a plan for you, too. And, even though the bee is small, what he does is not unimportant.

Lord, I choose to walk with You each step
and trust You for what happens. Amen.

MORNING

Lacking Nothing

Consider it pure joy, my brothers and sisters, whenever you face trials of many kinds, because you know that the testing of your faith produces perseverance.
JAMES 1:2–3 NIV

Trials don't get easier from one to the next. But when we get through one—battered but not broken—we can look back to see growth and strength, which we can take into the next. And we can walk straight ahead, knowing that in the end we will be mature and complete, lacking absolutely nothing in Christ Jesus.

Abba Father, I know You go with me through these trials. I know that any perseverance or strength I have is only because of You and Your faithfulness to me.

EVENING

Your Worst Enemy

I praise you, for I am fearfully and wonderfully made.
PSALM 139:14 ESV

Insecurity can spread like poison ivy. It will eat away at your confidence and affect how you view yourself. But your worth does not come from your outward appearance. Your worth comes from God, who—unlike beauty—is unchanging and permanent.

Father, please help me not to get discouraged by my appearance. I have confidence and value through You. I am beautiful in Your eyes. Amen.

Morning

Ezekiel Speaks to the Lost

Then He said to me, "Son of man, go to the house of Israel and speak with My words to them."
EZEKIEL 3:4 NASB

At times we are unwilling to risk presenting the Gospel message because of personal rejection. However, the outcome isn't our problem, it's God's. And He says the same thing to us that He did to Ezekiel: "But you shall speak My words to them whether they listen or not, for they are rebellious" (Ezekiel 2:7 NASB).

Lord, help me depend on Your Word to accomplish all You intend, by Your powerful Spirit.

Evening

Created for a Purpose

Always do your work well for the Lord. You know that whatever you do for Him will not be wasted.
1 CORINTHIANS 15:58 NLV

Knowing you have a purpose is like having a vision of where you're going. The Bible says that "if people can't see what God is doing, they stumble all over themselves" (Proverbs 29:18 MSG). But you won't stumble because you know God has a plan and a purpose. . .just for you.

Dear God, thank You for creating me with a purpose in mind.

Morning

The Secret of Serendipity

A happy heart makes the face cheerful.
Proverbs 15:13 NIV

A happy heart turns life's situations into opportunities for fun. For instance, if a storm snuffs out the electricity, light a candle and play games, tell stories, or just enjoy the quiet. When we seek innocent pleasures, we glean the benefits of a happy heart.

Dear Lord, Because of You, I have a happy heart.
Lead me to do something fun and spontaneous today! Amen.

Evening

An Overflowing Heart

The Lord *is my strength and my shield; my heart trusts in him,*
and he helps me. My heart leaps for joy, and with my song I praise him.
Psalm 28:7 NIV

Are you ever overcome with thankfulness for the blessings that God has poured out on your life? Living a life of gratitude will fill each day with joy!

God, thank You for helping me with my accomplishments.
My soul is full of joy. Thank You for Your many blessings. Amen.

DAY 202

Morning

Core Strength

He gives strength to the weary
and increases the power of the weak.
Isaiah 40:29 NIV

A strong spiritual core will help ensure that you remain stable and secure in a changing world. That you are able to keep from falling and that you are able to move and live gracefully. As you exercise your physical body, also make a commitment to regularly exercise your spiritual core as well.

Father, help me to return again and again to the core foundations of my spiritual health. Amen.

Evening

Do I Really Need It?

And my God will supply all your needs
according to His riches in glory in Christ Jesus.
Philippians 4:19 NASB

This world is not your home, and in heaven you'll be surrounded by the Lord's treasures. So store up your treasure in heaven, and know that God will supply what you truly need.

God, as I struggle with things that I want, help me to focus on others' needs and how I can help meet them. Help me to be thankful for everything I have and remember that You supply all my needs. Amen.

Morning

The Father's Voice

What use is it, my brethren, if someone says he has faith but he has no works? Can that faith save him?
James 2:14 NASB

Your heavenly Father is always listening, and as long as you follow His voice, He will guide you back to safety and into His loving arms.

God, help me to listen for Your voice and follow Your direction. Amen.

Evening

Forgiven? Forget!

Forgetting those things which are behind.
Philippians 3:13 NKJV

It can be so easy to dwell on past mistakes and failures. But that won't help your future. So dwell on the blessings of the Lord, not on your own past.

Dear God, I'm not strong enough to carry my past failures. Teach me to leave them in Your hands. Amen.

DAY
204

Morning

David's Family Tree

David. . .lay with her; and when she had purified herself from her uncleanness, she returned to her house. The woman conceived; and she sent and told David, and said, "I am pregnant."
2 Samuel 11:4–5 NASB

Although David should have accompanied his men into battle against the sons of Ammon, he instead stayed home. And there was beautiful Bathsheba, washing herself on her rooftop in the warmth of the evening. At any rate, David succumbed to temptation, and Bathsheba later realized she was with child.

Lord, help me to be accountable to You.

Evening

Bring Back the Sparkle

O Lord, how long will you forget me? Forever? . . .Turn and answer me, O Lord my God! Restore the sparkle to my eyes, or I will die.
Psalm 13:1, 3 NLT

God tells us in His Word that His ways are not our ways (Isaiah 55:8). His timing is perfect, and His plan for you is good. He is always working everything out for your good and His glory (Romans 8:28)—even when it doesn't seem like it.

God, please bring back the sparkle to my eyes—
the sparkle that comes from my hope in You.

MORNING

A Very Important Phrase

And it came to pass. . .
FOUND MORE THAN 400 TIMES IN THE KING JAMES BIBLE

Every day, week, and year are made up of things that "come to pass"—so even if we fail, we needn't be disheartened. Other opportunities—better days—will come. Let's look past those hard things today and glorify the name of the Lord.

Lord Jesus, how awesome it is that You send or allow these little things that will pass. May we recognize Your hand in them today and praise You for them.

EVENING

Resist!

Do not be overcome by evil,
but overcome evil with good.
ROMANS 12:21 NIV

In order to resist it and turn from the sin, you need to fill your life and your mind with holy and righteous things that will distract you from the temptation of sin. Your enemy will throw temptation at you, but it's your job to resist it. When you do that, sin will flee.

Dear God, help me resist sin and temptation
so I can stay rooted in Your truth. Amen.

DAY
206

Morning

The Bar Is Too High!

She gets up while it is still night; she provides food for her family. . . .
Her lamp does not go out at night.
Proverbs 31:15, 18 NIV

God wired each of us with different gifts, different energy levels, different responsibilities. Proverbs 31 casts a floodlight on *all* women—those gifted in business, in home life, as caregivers. This chapter displays how women undergird their families and their communities.

Father, thank You for the important women in my life. You made each one of us with gifts and abilities. May we be used to glorify You. Amen.

Evening

Call Yourself "Masterpiece"

For we are God's masterpiece. He has created us anew in Christ Jesus, so we can do the good things he planned for us long ago.
Ephesians 2:10 NLT

Today is a great day to start recognizing your value. Every day, remind yourself, "I was made by the Artist who paints only masterpieces. His brushstrokes set me apart from everyone else. He filled my personality with original colors. I am special to Him!"

God, thank You for painting me with such beauty!
I look forward to what You have planned for my life. Amen.

Morning

The White Knight

Then I will rejoice in the Lord.
I will be glad because he rescues me.
Psalm 35:9 NLT

Live your life—your whole life—by seeking daily joy in the Savior of your soul, Jesus Christ. And here's the best news of all: He's already done the rescuing by dying on the cross for our sins! He's the *true* white knight who secured your eternity in heaven.

Stop waiting; seek His face today!

Jesus, I praise You because You are the rescuer of my soul. Remind me of this fact when I'm looking for relief in other people and places.

Evening

Being Strong

Look to the Lord and his strength; seek his face always.
1 Chronicles 16:11 NIV

But God says we don't have to be strong on our own. If we look to Him, He'll be strong for us. He'll give us strength for all sorts of things we may face in this life.

Dear Father, help me be strong when I need to be. Remind me that You are always there, giving me strength when I ask for help.

DAY 208

Morning

Is Anyone Listening?

And I will ask the Father, and He will give you another Comforter (Counselor, Helper, Intercessor, Advocate, Strengthener, and Standby), that He may remain with you forever.
John 14:16 AMP

Our world is filled with noise and distractions. Look for a place where you can be undisturbed for a few minutes. Take a deep breath, lift your prayers, and listen. God will speak—and your heart will hear.

Dear Lord, I thank You for Your care.
Help me to recognize Your voice and to listen well.

Evening

God's Awesome Workmanship

Thank you for making me so wonderfully complex!
Your workmanship is marvelous—how well I know it.
Psalm 139:14 NLT

Not too long ago, God crafted you. He caused you to develop in a very safe place until the day you were born. In those few months, He fashioned your body and began its functions. He made you unique, with the qualities that make you the person you are.

Dear Jesus, thank You for making me according to Your plan.
Please help me to remember how special I am and how
marvelous Your works are. In Your name, amen.

Morning

A Comfortable Place

Don't you realize that your body is the temple of the Holy Spirit, who lives in you and was given to you by God? You do not belong to yourself.
1 Corinthians 6:19 NLT

Our bodies belong to God. They are a reflection to others of Him. Taking care of ourselves shows others that we honor God enough to respect and use wisely what He has given us.

Dear Lord, thank You for letting me belong to You. May my body be a comfortable place for You. Amen.

Evening

Can You Hear Me Now?

The Lord has heard my plea;
the Lord will answer my prayer.
Psalm 6:9 NLT

Did you know that God knows your voice? He really does! He created you and even keeps count of every hair on your head. He knows exactly who you are when you pray; and not only does He hear you, but He also listens to *everything* you have to say. It's all important to Him!

Dear Lord, thank You for hearing my prayers and listening to my voice. Help me to have more faith that You will answer my cries for help. Amen.

DAY
210

MORNING

Saul and Stephen

They went on stoning Stephen as he called on the Lord and said, "Lord Jesus, receive my spirit!"
ACTS 7:59 NASB

Have you ever committed an action so despicable that you can't imagine God could ever forgive you? Saul—who would soon be acclaimed as the fearless apostle Paul—had been persuaded by his own pious intentions to stamp out the Gospel's heresy. After the stoning of Stephen, Saul entered home after home and dragged Christians off to prison. Eventually God changed his heart and he began to spread the Gospel.

Thank You, God, for changing Saul into Paul!

EVENING

God Has Made a Way

Jesus said to him, "I am the way, the truth, and the life. No one comes to the Father except through Me."
JOHN 14:6 NKJV

Long before you were born, the Father made a way for you. He sent His only Son, Jesus, to die on a cross for your sins. Jesus is the only way to the Father. To know God and to spend eternity with Him in heaven, you must know His Son.

Come into my heart, Jesus, and forgive me of my sins. I want to follow You. Amen.

Morning

Complicated Relationships

And David said unto him, Fear not: for I will surely shew thee kindness for Jonathan thy father's sake, and will restore thee all the land of Saul thy father; and thou shalt eat bread at my table continually.
2 Samuel 9:7 KJV

In our own difficult relationships, loyalty and kindness may also seem an unwise response. But God wants our actions to always reflect His readiness to bless amid heartache and hurt.

Father, when forgiveness seems impossible,
help me act in accordance with Your unconditional love.

Evening

Jump In! The Water Is Just Fine

"But since you are like lukewarm water, neither hot nor cold, I will spit you out of my mouth!"
Revelation 3:16 NLT

Sin has a funny way of fooling you into thinking "it's okay" to sin a little, but the Bible says differently. In fact, it says that God wants to spit out a lukewarm Christian from His mouth. So don't get used to sin. You have to choose between the world's way and God's way.

Lord, please help me to stand my ground when it comes to my beliefs.

Morning

Judged!

A woman in that town who lived a sinful life. . .came there with an alabaster jar of perfume. As she stood behind him at his feet weeping, she began to wet his feet with her tears. Then she wiped them with her hair, kissed them and poured perfume on them.
Luke 7:37–38 NIV

We need not judge a casual acquaintance's spiritual life—God can do that. All we need to do is love, and He will bring blessings.

Thank You, Lord, that Your first reaction to me was love, not condemnation. Turn my heart in love to all who don't yet know You. Amen.

Evening

The Flip Side

"Do to others whatever you would like them to do to you. This is the essence of all that is taught in the law and the prophets."
Matthew 7:12 NLT

Jesus talks a lot about not judging others when we have sin in our own life that needs to be dealt with first (see Matthew 7:1–5). He wants us to love and be considerate of others, even if we might disagree sometimes. Ask God to help you respond to others in a way that would make Him smile.

God, please give me the courage to do the right thing.

Morning

Antichrist, the Ruler to Come

"In his place a despicable person will arise, on whom the honor of kingship has not been conferred, but he will come in a time of tranquility and seize the kingdom by intrigue."
Daniel 11:21 NASB

Jesus Himself warned the Jews about this diabolical person, telling them that when they saw him to "let those who are in Judea flee to the mountains" (Mark 13:14 AMP).

Lord, compel me with new urgency to study Your powerful Word, that I might bring it to others.

Evening

Life Everlasting

"For God so loved the world that He gave His only begotten Son, that whoever believes in Him should not perish but have everlasting life."
John 3:16 NKJV

Our eternal life is where our focus should be—even now!—and we should always be looking forward to that day when we meet Jesus face-to-face. God wanted us to have a life with Him so much that He gave His only Son, Jesus, to die that we might live!

Dear God, please help me keep my focus on the life that truly matters, the eternal life I will have someday because of Your amazing gift. Amen.

DAY
214

Morning

One Thing Is Needed

"Martha, Martha," the Lord answered. "You are worried and upset about many things. But only one thing is needed."
LUKE 10:41–42 NIRV

Since God has blessed each of us with twenty-four hours, let's seek His direction on how to spend this invaluable commodity, wisely—giving more to people than things, spending more time on relationships than the rat race. In Luke, our Lord reminded dear, dogged, drained Martha that only one thing is needed—Him.

Father God, help me to use my time wisely. Open my eyes to see what is truly important.

Evening

Growing Up Gorgeous

And the LORD God planted a garden.
GENESIS 2:8 KJV

Plants left to themselves don't remain lovely for long. They are eventually choked by weeds, devoured by insects, or crushed by careless feet. You're far better off submitting to the hands of your wise and loving Creator than trying to develop on your own. Have patience, little blossom. It may be a lot of work, but God's flowers always grow up gorgeous!

Lord, You make all things beautiful. Help me to be patient and submissive while You cultivate me into a blossom worthy of Your love. Amen.

MORNING

Confident Persistence

"Don't be afraid. Just stand still and watch the LORD rescue you today. The Egyptians you see today will never be seen again."
EXODUS 14:13 NLT

When you become bewildered and petrified with fear, "don't be afraid. Just stand still and watch the LORD rescue you *today*," because the problems, frustrations, and barriers you see today will never be seen again (emphasis added). Be persistent, and God will see you through.

Lord, be my shield. Surround me with Your presence. Help me to keep still in this situation and watch You see me through it.

EVENING

Replace Judging with Loving

"For in the same way you judge others, you will be judged, and with the measure you use, it will be measured to you."
MATTHEW 7:2 NIV

When you judge someone without understanding his or her situation, you'll often be put in a very similar situation during your lifetime. Sometimes God allows things like that to happen so that you can understand and forgive those toward whom you harbor bitter feelings.

Dear God, help me not to avoid people I don't understand, and please give me wisdom to know how to act around them.

DAY
216

MORNING

Answered Knee-Mail

The prayer of a righteous person is powerful and effective.
JAMES 5:16 NIV

Prayer isn't just a way to seek protection and guidance; it's how we develop a deeper relationship with our heavenly Father. We can access this power anywhere. We don't need a wi-fi hot spot or a high-speed modem. We just need to look up. He's connected and waiting.

Father, thank You for being at my side all the time.
Help me to turn to You instantly, in need and in praise. Amen.

EVENING

Your Future

"For I know the plans I have for you," declares the LORD, "plans to prosper you and not to harm you, plans to give you hope and a future."
JEREMIAH 29:11 NIV

The Bible says if you commit whatever you do to the Lord, your plans will succeed (Proverbs 16:3). As you plan your future, ask God to guide your choices. Let Him know that you want His plan to be *your* plan for the future. Then you'll have it made in the shade!

Dear God, I choose to go along with Your
plan because I want Your best for me. Amen.

MORNING

Who Helps the Helper?

The LORD is my strength and my shield; my heart trusted in him, and I am helped: therefore my heart greatly rejoiceth; and with my song will I praise him.
PSALM 28:7 KJV

Who helps the helper? The Lord does. When we are weak, He is strong. When we are vulnerable, He is our shield. When we can no longer trust in our own resources, we can trust in Him.

Father, I'm worn out. I can't care for all the people and needs You bring into my life by myself. I need Your strength. Thank You for being my helper and my shield.

EVENING

Rest and Trust

And my God will meet all your needs according to the riches of his glory in Christ Jesus.
PHILIPPIANS 4:19 NIV

Sometimes when people are afraid and they don't believe God will take care of them, they try to push God out of the driver's seat of their lives by telling Him what to do and how to treat them. God says He will take care of all our needs, so we can rest, trust, and let Him drive our lives. There is no need to fear.

Lord, thank You that You take care of all my needs, big and small.

MORNING

Magnifying Life

My soul makes its boast in the LORD; let the humble hear and be glad.
Oh, magnify the LORD with me, and let us exalt his name together!
PSALM 34:2–3 ESV

Does your life make Christ larger and easier for others to see? Maybe you can't honestly say you desire this. Start there. Confess that. Ask Him to remind you of His favor and to work humility into your life, to help you pray like the psalmist did.

Christ Jesus, help me to remember what You have done for me and desire for others to see and know You.

EVENING

Cowardly Lion or Courageous Woman?

Therefore, being always of good courage, and knowing that while
we are at home in the body we are absent from the Lord—
for we walk by faith, not by sight—we are of good courage.
2 CORINTHIANS 5:6–8 NASB

Take courage in every situation. The possibilities are endless when you draw on courage from the Lord.

God, sometimes I'm so scared of trying something new, or even doing what's right. Please help me to see that You have given me courage and I don't have to be afraid. Amen.

Morning

But What about the Jews?

For what does the Scripture say? "Abraham believed God, and it was credited to Him as righteousness."
Romans 4:3 NASB

God made Abraham, the one the Jews claim as their father, a promise—and he believed God. His belief wasn't merely an intellectual assent. The reason that Abraham could place his trust in God was because God kept His promises. No matter how impossible the situation looks, God always comes through.

I thank You that I worship a God whose word can be trusted. I know Jesus will always be there for me.

Evening

Hope Giver

Do any of the worthless idols of the nations bring rain? Do the skies themselves send down showers? No, it is you, Lord our God. Therefore our hope is in you, for you are the one who does all this.
Jeremiah 14:22 NIV

Jesus is only a prayer away, and He alone can calm your fears and the storm.

Lord, thank You for my family. And thank You for giving me hope, even in situations that seem hopeless!

DAY 220

Morning

No More Sting

O death, where is thy sting?
O grave, where is thy victory?
1 Corinthians 15:55 KJV

We have a choice to make. We can either live life in fear or live life by faith. Jesus Christ has conquered our greatest fear—death. He rose victorious and has given us eternal life through faith. Knowing this truth enables us to courageously face our fears. There is no fear that cannot be conquered by faith.

Lord, You alone know my fears. Help me to trust You more.
May I walk in the victory that You have purchased for me. Amen.

Evening

God Understands

Be ye doers of the word, and not hearers only.
James 1:22 KJV

It's so easy to talk the talk and say whatever sounds good. It's completely different to actually carry through and make a change in our actions. Even though change is hard, God can help do it.

Dear Father, show me how to change my actions, not just speak empty words.

Morning

Understand. . .Then Act

Make the most of every opportunity in these evil days.
Don't act thoughtlessly, but understand what the Lord wants you to do.
Ephesians 5:16–17 NLT

Are you an actor or a reactor? Are you a thinker or a knee-jerker? The Lord longs for us to think before we act or speak—to act on His behalf. To react takes little or no thought, but to live a life that reflects the image of Christ takes lots of work!

Lord, I don't want to be a reactor. Today I give You my knee-jerking tendencies. Guard my words and actions, Father.

Evening

Knock, Knock!

Be anxious for nothing, but in everything by prayer and supplication with thanksgiving let your requests be made known to God. And the peace of God, which surpasses all comprehension, will guard your hearts and your minds in Christ Jesus.
Philippians 4:6–7 NASB

God tells us *not* to worry—*not* to be anxious—but to come to Him in prayer with thanksgiving. You can call on the name of the Lord with confidence—and thankfulness!—that He hears you.

Father, I'm so thankful that I can call out to You with the assurance that You hear me—and help me!

DAY 222

MORNING

Well Watered

"The LORD will guide you always; he will satisfy your needs in a sun-scorched land and will strengthen your frame. You will be like a well-watered garden, like a spring whose waters never fail."
ISAIAH 58:11 NIV

We need a downpour of God's Word and the Holy Spirit's presence in our parched spirit. This comes from consistent Bible study, the necessary pruning of confessed sin, and prayer time. These create a life to which others are drawn to come and linger in His refreshing presence.

Eternal Father, strengthen my frame, guide my paths, and satisfy my needs as only You can. Make my life a well-watered garden, fruitful for You and Your purposes. Amen.

EVENING

My Future

Do not conform to the pattern of this world, but be transformed by the renewing of your mind. Then you will be able to test and approve what God's will is—his good, pleasing and perfect will.
ROMANS 12:2 NIV

We may not know the details of our future, but we can be assured about God's most important plan. He wants to make us beautiful in spirit. And He will do what He needs to do to bring about that plan.

Dear Father, thank You for making good plans for my future. Help me to fulfill Your plans by becoming more like You.

MORNING

What Is Your Request?

And pray in the Spirit on all occasions with all kinds of prayers and requests. With this in mind, be alert and always keep on praying.
EPHESIANS 6:18 NIV

But be patient. What we may view as a nonanswer may simply be God saying, *"Wait"* or *"I have something better for you."* He *will* answer. Keep in mind that His ways are not our ways, nor are His thoughts our thoughts.

Father God, here are my needs. I lay them at Your feet, walking away unburdened and assured that You have it all under control. Thank You!

EVENING

My Strength Comes from God

"Don't panic. I'm with you. There's no need to fear for I'm your God. I'll give you strength. I'll help you. I'll hold you steady, keep a firm grip on you."
ISAIAH 41:10 MSG

Remember that God is with you in every situation—offering you His strength when you need to be strong, to help you stand up for what is right. Lean on Him. He will always give you the courage to do what is right.

Dear God, please help me to trust that You are always in my corner, keeping me strong and steady.

DAY 224

MORNING

Peace Despite Our Trials

For while we were still helpless,
at the right time Christ died for the ungodly.
ROMANS 5:6 NASB

People have scoured every nook and cranny of the globe in search of peace. From yoga and transcendental meditation to new-age tranquillity tapes and self-empowerment courses, people will try just about anything. But do these methods work?

Of course not!

Lord, I know the only true and lasting peace comes from Jesus Christ.

EVENING

A Mega Bestseller

All Scripture is God-breathed and is useful for teaching,
rebuking, correcting and training in righteousness.
2 TIMOTHY 3:16 NIV

God was faithful to the ancient people of the Bible, just as He is faithful to you today. Not only can you learn from the people you meet in the Bible, but also, God's Word is a mega bestseller—and it's helpful for guidance in everything that matters most in life.

Lord, please give me the desire to read Your living Word,
the Bible, so that I might grow strong in my faith. Amen.

Morning

A Better Offer

"So in everything, do to others what
you would have them do to you."
Matthew 7:12 NIV

How do you treat friends, colleagues, and acquaintances? Do you remain committed to your responsibilities? What are your priorities? God, upon request, will help us prioritize our commitments so that our "yes" is "yes" and our "no" is "no." Then in everything we do, we are liberated to do to others as we would have them do to us.

Lord, please prioritize my commitments to enable me in everything to do to others as I would desire for them to do to me. Amen.

Evening

But You Promised!

God's way is perfect. All the Lord*'s promises prove true.*
Psalm 18:30 NLT

The thing about promises is they are no good unless they're kept. God *always* keeps His promises, but sometimes we get tired of waiting for them to come true. We want God's promises on *our* time instead of trusting Him for His perfect timing. And in our selfishness, we run out of patience.

Jesus, please help me to have patience. I want to wait for all the good and wonderful promises You have for me.

DAY 226

Morning

Anxieties

Casting the whole of your care [all your anxieties, all your worries, all your concerns, once and for all] on Him, for He cares for you affectionately and cares about you watchfully.
1 Peter 5:7 AMP

Because He cares for you. Not because you have to. Not because it's the "right" thing to do. Not because it's what you're supposed to do. No. Read it again. . . . Because He cares for you. That's right, He cares for you!

Father, I am overjoyed at Your concern for me. Please teach me to cast my cares into Your arms. . .and leave them there.

Evening

Make the Best of It

For you know that when your faith is tested, your endurance has a chance to grow.
James 1:3 NLT

Here's what you need to focus on instead: When you're facing difficult situations, Jesus Himself will come alongside you to help you through it. He will give you peace, and you will feel closer to God during the hard stuff (see Psalm 34:18)! Praise Him!

God, please give me the strength to make the best of everything I face in life.

Morning

Put On a Happy Face

He restoreth my soul: he leadeth me in the paths of righteousness for his name's sake.
Psalm 23:3 KJV

Be encouraged. The Lord has promised He hears our pleas and knows our situations. He will never leave us. He will guide us through our difficulties and beyond them. In *Streams in the Desert*, Mrs. Charles E. Cowman states, "Every misfortune, every failure, every loss may be transformed. God has the power to transform all misfortunes into 'God-sends.' "

Father, I'm down in the dumps today. You are my unending source of strength. Gather me in Your arms for always. Amen.

Evening

More Than Just Muscles

In your strength I can crush an army; with my God I can scale any wall.
Psalm 18:29 NLT

God has given you unique strengths so that you can overcome the challenges that come your way. It won't always be easy. Even strong people will have moments of weakness, but you have a partner and friend in God.

God, please show me each of my strengths. I want to be able to use them to fulfill the purpose You have for me.

DAY
228

Morning

Hold On!

Let us not become weary in doing good, for at the proper time we will reap a harvest if we do not give up.
GALATIANS 6:9 NIV

Have you ever felt that God abandoned you? Do you feel your labor is in vain and no one appreciates the sacrifices you have made? When we come to the end of our rope, God ties a knot.

Dear Lord, help me when I can no longer help myself. Banish my discouragement and give me the rest and restoration I need so that I might hear Your voice. Amen.

Evening

That You May Know

I write these things to you who believe in the name of the Son of God so that you may know that you have eternal life.
1 JOHN 5:13 NIV

When writing the book of 1 John, the apostle did not say, "I write these things to you who believe in the name of the Son of God so that you may *hope* that you have eternal life." He wrote, inspired by God, ". . .that you may *know* that you have eternal life" (emphasis added).

Thank You, God, that I know I have eternal life through Jesus. Amen.

Morning

Safety Net

*Therefore there is now no condemnation
for those who are in Christ Jesus.*
Romans 8:1 NASB

God's rules provide for us a huge safety net. When we bounce against its sides, we become aware of the need to change our direction.

I rejoice that I am a child of God and heir to the kingdom! Hallelujah!

Evening

On Earth, in Heaven

*"If I go and prepare a place for you, I will come back and
take you to be with me that you also may be where I am."*
John 14:3 NIV

Throughout the days that God has appointed for us to live on the earth, we are to live for the Lord. What we do here should be for the purpose of pointing others toward Him. And then, when our days here are done, we will be united with our Savior to begin our forever with Him.

Dear Father, help me to remember that this life is not the end.

DAY
230

Morning

Be Still, My Soul

Be still in the presence of the Lord,
and wait patiently for him to act.
Psalm 37:7 NLT

God asks us to quiet our spirits before Him, to submit to His will for us. As people of God, we wait expectantly for Him to work all things for our good and His glory (Romans 8:28).

Father, may I quiet my soul before You today. Help me to see Your loving hand in every difficulty I face, knowing that You are accomplishing Your purposes in me.

Evening

Gone Fishin'

"Come, follow me," Jesus said,
"and I will send you out to fish for people."
Matthew 4:19 NIV

Chances are, if you're fishing for compliments, you're too focused on yourself. It's time to take your eyes off yourself and get them back onto God. Because if you need the praise of others to feel good about yourself, you're probably pretty empty inside. You need a God refill. Ask Him to fill you with His love and His confidence today, and become a fisher of people, not compliments.

God, help me to take my eyes off myself
and put them back onto You. Amen.

MORNING

DAY 231

One Step at a Time

With your help I can advance against a troop;
with my God I can scale a wall.
PSALM 18:29 NIV

We often become discouraged when we face a mountain-size task. Whether it's weight loss or a graduate degree or our income taxes, some things just seem impossible. And they often *can't* be done—not all at once. Tasks like these are best faced one step at a time. One pound at a time. Chipping away instead of moving the whole mountain at once.

Dear Father, the task before me seems impossible but with your help, I know I can break the task into smaller, manageable goals. Give me your wisdom and strength to conquer all that is before me. Amen.

EVENING

Hungry for Love

But you, Lord, are a compassionate and gracious God,
slow to anger, abounding in love and faithfulness.
PSALM 86:15 NIV

When you are hungry for love, remember God loves you more than anyone can. Also remember that He created a "love hole" inside of you that He wants to fill with Himself. He created you to give and receive love to others, but no matter how well others love you, there will always be an empty place inside you that can only be filled by Jesus.

Lord Jesus, I want and need love. I thank You that You made me for love.

DAY
232

MORNING

Peace through Prayer

And the peace of God, which surpasses all understanding, will guard your hearts and minds through Christ Jesus.
PHILIPPIANS 4:7 NKJV

The peace of God cannot be explained. It cannot be bought. The world cannot give it to us. But when we release our cares to the Lord in prayer, His peace washes over us and fills our hearts and minds. What a comfort is the peace of God when we find ourselves in the valley.

Sovereign God, You are with me through the good and the bad. Draw near to me and replace my worry with Your peace. Amen.

EVENING

Getting to Know You

I'm amazed at how well you know me. It's more than I can understand.
PSALM 139:6 NIRV

Do you ever feel like no one really "gets" you? Like, they don't understand what makes you tick? Maybe that's because we often hide the real us from people, afraid that if they really knew us they wouldn't like us.

Not a lot of people really know the real me, Lord, the woman on the inside. I'm so glad You do! Thank You for taking the time to know me. . .inside and out! Amen.

Morning

Silence

He was oppressed, and he was afflicted,
yet he opened not his mouth.
Isaiah 53:7 ESV

The Father can speak; we can listen. We can speak, knowing He is listening. Trust is built in silence, and confidence strengthens in silence.

Lord Jesus, help me to learn from Your silence. Help me to trust You more so that I don't feel the need to explain myself. Give me the desire and the courage to be alone with You and learn to hear Your voice.

Evening

He's Got Your Back

"In the world you will have tribulation.
But take heart; I have overcome the world."
John 16:33 ESV

If you wake up *every* morning knowing that God will take care of you in *every* circumstance, there will be nothing to fear. The meanest coworker, the hardest project, the roughest day—none of it can separate you from His love and protection. He's got your back.

Father, thank You for watching over me and giving me strength when I ask for it. Help me not to be afraid or anxious when life throws new and difficult things my way. Amen.

DAY
234

Morning

Paul's Prayer for the Jews

Brethren, my heart's desire and my prayer
to God for them is for their salvation.
Romans 10:1 NASB

Is the deepest concern of your heart that those whom you love will share heaven with Christ? The deepest longing of Paul's soul was that the Jews might know their Messiah. Paul longed for the Israelites, "to whom belongs the adoption as sons, and the glory and the covenants and the giving of the Law and the temple service and the promises" (Romans 9:4–5 NASB), to understand that Christ had come to save them.

Lord, clarify Your Word, that my loved ones may yield in faith.

Evening

Attitude Is Everything

Not looking to your own interests but each of you to the interests of the others.
In your relationships with one another, have the same mindset as Christ Jesus.
Philippians 2:4–5 NIV

No matter what happens to you, you are always in charge of your attitude. The Bible wants our attitudes to be like Jesus' attitude: He was humble, He put others above Himself, and He was obedient to God (Philippians 2:7).

Dear Lord, please change my attitude to be more like Yours.
Help me to be humble and be a servant to You and others.

MORNING

A Fresh Perspective

"Listen now to me and I will give you
some advice, and may God be with you."
EXODUS 18:19 NIV

What is there about your present situation that might require perspective from someone else? Is there something you could be doing differently? Is there a task you could be delegating or an option you haven't considered? Learn from Moses—take the advice of someone who could offer you a much-needed perspective.

Heavenly Father, I thank You for the perspective that others can bring. Teach me to listen to and heed wise advice.

EVENING

Fresh Water

And the Scriptures give us hope and encouragement
as we wait patiently for God's promises to be fulfilled.
ROMANS 15:4 NLT

The Word of God is like fish food for your soul, and your spirit cannot grow in relationship with God in cloudy water. Each day, you need to sprinkle fresh food into your life by reading the Bible and thinking about what it says. When you apply it, you'll get answers for your questions and help for your struggles.

Dear God, help me remember to study the Bible every day.

DAY 236

MORNING

Lady Wisdom Gives Directions

Does not wisdom cry out, and understanding lift up her voice? She takes her stand on the top of the high hill, beside the way, where the paths meet.
PROVERBS 8:1–2 NKJV

Wisdom longs to make a difference in our stressful experiences that sometimes lead to destruction. She never stops sharing her vital message: whoever heeds God's instruction gains more than silver, gold, or rubies. His truth, His directions lead listeners to life.

Father, help us shake off the hypnotizing effects of our culture's values and listen to Your wisdom.

EVENING

The Perfect Road Map

I will give thanks to You, for I am fearfully and wonderfully made. . . . And in Your book were all written the days that were ordained for me.
PSALM 139:14, 16 NASB

Some days you may question why on earth you are here. What's the purpose of your life? Well, rest in the assurance that God has a plan. A beautiful plan. An incredible plan. And He wants to see you succeed in it. You don't have to have all the answers right now.

God, remind me not to worry about the future but to rely totally on You. Amen.

Morning

Esther Is Chosen

"Then let the young lady who pleases the king be queen in place of Vashti."
ESTHER 2:4 NASB

The book of Esther is a beautiful story of a woman's absolute faith and trust in her God. God placed Esther in a position of authority—in order to save the people of Israel.

In the beginning, Esther was unaware of how God would use her life. Lord, let me be as available and obedient to You.

Evening

The God of Hope

May the God of hope fill you with all joy and peace as you trust in him, so that you may overflow with hope by the power of the Holy Spirit.
ROMANS 15:13 NIV

Being a Christian doesn't always shield you from bad situations. The difference between you and the nonbeliever is that when bad stuff happens you have hope. Everything is possible with God. Nothing is too hard for Him.

Dear God, You are the God of the impossible. I put all my hope and trust in You.

DAY
238

Morning

Mirror Image

Behold, thou art fair, my love; behold,
thou art fair; thou hast doves' eyes.
Song of Solomon 1:15 KJV

When God looks at us as Christians, He sees the reflection of Christ. He sees us as very beautiful. God loves to behold us when we are covered in Christ. The image He sees has none of the blemishes or imperfections, only the beauty.

Oh God, thank You for beholding me as being fair and valuable.
Help me to see myself through Your eyes. Amen.

Evening

Choose Your Own Adventure

To choose life is to love the Lord *your God,*
obey him, and stay close to him.
Deuteronomy 30:20 NCV

God's will doesn't have to be very complicated. It's just making a series of right choices. If you decide to follow after God and you try to make choices that honor Him, you'll be seeking after God's will in Your life and headed down the right path. What a great adventure!

Dear God, please help me to make good choices.
I want to live my life for You. Thanks for this great adventure!

MORNING

Good Works Are All Around

Well reported of for good works; if [a widow] have brought up children, if she have lodged strangers, if she have washed the saints' feet, if she have relieved the afflicted, if she have diligently followed every good work.
1 TIMOTHY 5:10 KJV

Good work is not a mystery that we have to meditate to find. We just need to see the needs around us and meet them as God gives us the strength and resources to do so.

That's practical—and pure—Christianity.

Father, help me to see and follow the good works that are within my reach.

EVENING

What's Your Attitude?

I pray that from his glorious, unlimited resources he will empower you with inner strength through his Spirit.
EPHESIANS 3:16 NLT

You can tear down your walls by opening your heart to positive attitudes, and God can then add strength, joy, and peace to your life. It takes practice to turn off the negative thinking, but you can do it with God's help. Just remember He is always there, waiting to give you the strength you need. Strong is good. God's strength is better.

Heavenly Father, thank You for giving me Your power and strength to do all things. Amen.

DAY 240

Morning

The Martha Syndrome

"My dear Martha, you are worried and upset over all these details! There is only one thing worth being concerned about. Mary has discovered it, and it will not be taken away from her."
Luke 10:41–42 NLT

It's very easy to create a life jam-packed with responsibilities and commitments with no time to enjoy any of it or seek fellowship with the Father. If you find yourself worried and upset, like Martha, take some time out and decide what is really important.

Jesus, I want to be like Mary, patiently and expectantly sitting at Your feet in relationship with You.

Evening

God Listens

But God has surely listened and has heard my prayer.
Psalm 66:19 NIV

Sometimes when we pray, it feels like our words bounce off the ceiling and right back down into our hearts. We wonder if God is listening. We wonder if He can even hear us. But the Bible tells us that God does listen. He loves us, and He cares about what we have to say.

Dear Father, I'm sorry for the times I've sinned. I know You hear me. Thank You for always listening.

Morning

Build for Today

*"Build homes, and plan to stay. Plant gardens,
and eat the food they produce."*
Jeremiah 29:5 NLT

God wants us to live for today. We can't allow dreams for tomorrow to paralyze our lives today. God's presence enables us to live in the present.

Dear heavenly Father, You have given us the gift of today. You want us to plant gardens and make homes. Show us joy and fulfillment in the present. Amen.

Evening

He Is Strong

*"For the eyes of the Lord range throughout the earth to
strengthen those whose hearts are fully committed to him."*
2 Chronicles 16:9 NIV

There is good news. You don't have to be the strong one. The Bible tells us in 2 Chronicles that God is *always* looking for His children in need of strength. He wants to be your strength. Call on Him. Tell God where you are weak, and ask Him to be strong in your place.

*I am weak, Lord, but how wonderful
to know that You are strong! Amen.*

DAY
242

Morning

Hearing God's Spirit Speak

Now we have received, not the spirit of the world, but the Spirit who is from God, so that we may know the things freely given to us by God.
1 Corinthians 2:12 NASB

Here's an excuse heard often: "We can't try to interpret the Bible ourselves because we'll get confused." But to refuse the Holy Spirit the opportunity to instruct you, as He promised He would, is to refuse true understanding.

Lord, fill my mind and heart with true understanding.

Evening

God's Got This!

Those who listen to instruction will prosper;
those who trust the Lord will be joyful.
Proverbs 16:20 NLT

It's time to trust the Lord! He knows how you feel! He planned your life journey to include experiences where you will do your best to prepare, without an immediate guarantee you'll get the results you want. In these moments, you need to force yourself to depend on Him to take you the rest of the way. Let go, then celebrate and say, "God's got this!"

God, I want to give You everything that is troubling me today.

MORNING

Delightful Study

Great are the works of the LORD*;*
they are pondered by all who delight in them.
PSALM 111:2 NIV

Your delight in God's creation is a gift from Him and an offering of praise back to Him for what He has done. To be thankful for the interest God gives you in creation brings glory to Him and leads to knowing and appreciating Him more.

Great God of all creation, Giver of all good things, thank You for the endless beauty and wisdom in the world around me that speaks of You.

EVENING

Jesus Knows Me—I Am His!

"I am the good shepherd, and I know My own and My own know Me."
JOHN 10:14 NASB

God gave man free will—the ability to choose right or wrong (Genesis 3). You can *choose* to follow His ways and standards, or you can *choose* to rebel against them (see 1 John 2:15–17).

He chose you (John 15:16), and if you accepted Jesus as your Savior, you answered His call.

Lord, I know I'm Yours—help me not to listen to the temptations of this world, but Your voice and Your voice alone.

DAY
244

Morning

Stop and Consider

"Listen to this, Job; stop and consider God's wonders."
Job 37:14 NIV

"Stop and consider My wonders," God told Job. Then He pointed to ordinary observations of the natural world surrounding Job—the clouds that hung poised in the sky, the flashes of lightning. "Not so very ordinary" was God's lesson. Maybe He was trying to remind us that there is no such thing as ordinary. Let's open our eyes and see the wonders around us.

O Father, teach me to stop and consider the ordinary moments of my life as reminders of You.

Evening

Give Me Peace

I love the LORD, for he heard my voice; he heard my cry for mercy. Because he turned his ear to me, I will call on him as long as I live.
Psalm 116:1–2 NIV

You call out to God to give you the rest and peace that you really could use right about now. You then snuggle back under the covers, and it doesn't take long for you to doze off. Peace, peace, peace.

God, I know You hear my prayers. Help me not to forget You are always here for me. Amen.

MORNING

Jesus' Wristwatch

Look carefully then how you walk, not as unwise but as wise, making the best use of the time, because the days are evil.
EPHESIANS 5:15–16 ESV

Time is money, they say. Society preaches the value of making good use of our time—and the expense of wasting it.

In the Bible, Ephesians 5 speaks of using every opportunity wisely. But even though scripture teaches the value of time, Jesus never wore a watch. He didn't view His opportunities within the bounds of earthly time.

Father, help me to see where You are working and join You there.

EVENING

Saying Grace

I will praise him among the multitude.
PSALM 109:30 KJV

It's always uncomfortable to feel like an oddball. Unless all your friends are Christians who also pray for their food, you may feel a little uncomfortable doing so. But saying grace before meals is not just a family-around-the-dinner-table thing. And thanking God in public opens the door for you to witness to your unbelieving friends.

Dear God, thank You for all my blessings, including the food I eat. Give me courage to praise You publicly, even if others think I'm weird. Amen.

DAY
246

Morning

Our Bodies, God's Temple

*Do you not know that you are a temple of God,
and that the Spirit of God dwells in you?*
1 Corinthians 3:16 NASB

While people were living out the Old Testament times, God dwelled in His tabernacle. When God's Son, Jesus Christ, came to earth, He fulfilled God's requirements for sinful man through His death on the cross. Now God could cleanse man that He might indwell him, for God's temple is to be a holy place.

Lord, let me live as though I believe You are permeating my very being. Amen.

Evening

Protection from Danger

This I declare about the Lord: *He alone is my refuge,
my place of safety; he is my God, and I trust him.*
Psalm 91:2 NLT

God has offered Himself as a safe place in times of danger. He is like a place of safety in a storm. When His child looks for a place to run and hide, God opens His arms wide and provides a comfortable place to wait out the storm.

Dear Father, thank You for being a safe place for me.

MORNING

Rejoicing with Friends

"Then he calls his friends and neighbors together and says, 'Rejoice with me; I have found my lost sheep.' "
LUKE 15:6 NIV

God loves a good party, especially one that celebrates family togetherness. Just like the good shepherd in today's verse, He throws a pretty awesome party in heaven whenever a lost child returns to the fold. Celebrating comes naturally to Him, and—since you're created in His image—to you, too!

Lord, thank You for Your many blessings. And today I especially want to thank You for giving me friends to share my joys and sorrows.

EVENING

Adored

And I am convinced that nothing can ever separate us from God's love.
ROMANS 8:38 NLT

Did you realize that God adores you? He's crazy about you, and nothing you do can change the way He feels! He won't give you up, no matter what! In fact, He cares so much about you that He doesn't like to be away from you, even for a few minutes. He hopes you feel the same way about Him.

Lord, I know that You adore me, even when I mess up. I'm so relieved!

DAY
248

Morning

Did God Say. . . ?

For we walk by faith, not by sight.
2 Corinthians 5:7 nasb

As we learn to become more and more dependent on God, we trust Him more and more. Our faith, though it may have begun as the size of a mustard seed, will grow into a mighty tree.

Lord, I thank You for choosing me to work with You. Give me the faith I need to see Your hand in everyday circumstances and to ask You for the help I need.

Evening

My Protector

You protect me with salvation-armor; you hold me up with a firm hand, caress me with your gentle ways.
Psalm 18:35 msg

Every day and always, you have God. He protects you from every kind of evil. And if you let Him, God will even protect you from yourself and the things you might do—the wrong choices you might make that would bring you harm. Remember He is always there. Turn to Him instead of thinking you can protect yourself.

Dear God, thank You for always watching over me, always knowing what might happen before I do.

MORNING

Persistently Presented Petitions

"O woman, great is your faith! Let it be to you as you desire."
MATTHEW 15:28 NKJV

When our loved ones are troubled—emotionally, spiritually, financially, physically, mentally—our hearts are heavy and we feel helpless. But with Christ's ear within reach of our voice, we are anything but powerless. We have an interceder, someone to whom we can continually go and present our petitions.

God, I come to You, bringing the concerns of others. Lord, have mercy! Help these people in their hour of need. Amen.

EVENING

A Love Letter to Open

Jesus answered, "It is written: 'Man shall not live on bread alone, but on every word that comes from the mouth of God.' "
MATTHEW 4:4 NIV

God has given you a love letter. It's called the Bible. It's the main way you can hear Him speak to you. It's a light for you to know what to do in your life—and it's the most beautiful love letter ever written.

Lord, I want to know You better. Help me to spend time getting to know You through Your love letter to me. Amen.

DAY
250

Morning

God, Judge of Immorality Past and Present

Nor let us act immorally, as some of them did,
and twenty-three thousand fell in one day.
1 Corinthians 10:8 NASB

How can we stop ourselves from falling into sin? By remembering: "No temptation has overtaken you but such as is common to man; and God is faithful, who will not allow you to be tempted beyond what you are able, but with the temptation will provide the way of escape also, that you will be able to endure it" (1 Corinthians 10:13 NASB).

Father, help me avoid temptation by taking one step closer to You.

Evening

The Best Kind of Friends

One who loves a pure heart and who speaks
with grace will have the king for a friend.
Proverbs 22:11 NIV

Did you know that Jesus had people upset with Him all the time? That's a good reminder to us all that we cannot please everybody. Even Jesus didn't do that. He doesn't want us to please everyone—just Him! God doesn't want you to be a people pleaser; He wants you to be a Jesus pleaser!

God, help me to do my best to please You and not
worry about what other people think or say about me.

MORNING

Desperate Faith

And He said to her, "Daughter, your faith has made you well. Go in peace, and be healed of your affliction."
MARK 5:34 NKJV

We prefer to trust in the Lord along with our own understanding of how things should work out. Though we are given minds to read, think, and reason, ultimately our faith comes from abandoning hope in ourselves and risking all on Jesus.

Lord, I am often blind to my own weakness and my need of You. Help me to trust You the way this sick woman did.

EVENING

Watch Your Words

"For the mouth speaks what the heart is full of."
LUKE 6:45 NIV

Start choosing and using your words wisely! Look for opportunities to encourage your friends, family, coworkers, and strangers. Just think—your positive comment may be the only positive comment that person hears all week. Make a difference with your mouth today!

God, help me to be a builder with my words, not one who tears down. Amen.

DAY
252

Morning

Why Me?

I am Alpha and Omega, the beginning and the ending, saith the Lord, which is, and which was, and which is to come, the Almighty.
Revelation 1:8 KJV

When God spoke our world into existence, He called into being a certain reality, knowing then everything that ever was to happen—and everyone who ever was to be. That you exist now is cause for rejoicing! God made *you* to fellowship with Him!

Father, I thank You for giving me this difficult time in my life. Shine through all my trials today. I want You to get the glory.

Evening

Life's Not Fair

"Is he not the One...who shows no partiality to princes and does not favor the rich over the poor, for they are all the work of his hands?"
Job 34:18–19 NIV

God cares just as much for the starving child as He does for you. Today, ask God where He can use you to help those who are suffering. Perhaps letting you bless others was part of His plan all along.

Lord, it breaks my heart to know that some people have to suffer. Please help me see where You can use me to make a difference. Amen.

Morning

Faith, the Emotional Balancer

No man is justified by the law in the sight of God,
it is evident: for, The just shall live by faith.
Galatians 3:11 KJV

The Bible instructs us to live by faith—not by feelings. Faith assures us that daylight will dawn in our darkest moments, affirming God's presence so that even when we fail to pray and positive feelings fade, our moods surrender to song.

Heavenly Father, I pray for balance in my hide-under-the-covers days,
so that I might surrender to You in song. Amen.

Evening

I Am Not Alone

The Lord is near to all who call upon Him.
Psalm 145:18 NASB

Just remember that you are never. . .*never* alone. Because you are a child of the King, He promises never to leave you. And the more you communicate with Him, the closer you will feel to Him. So don't give up. Don't give in. Even if the world turns its back on you, remember that you have the God of the universe with you wherever you go.

Lord, it's hard when I feel alone, but I know
that You understand better than anyone else.

DAY 254

Morning

The Holy Spirit, Our Great Gift

Therefore I make known to you that no one speaking by the Spirit of God says, "Jesus is accursed"; and no one can say, "Jesus is Lord," except by the Holy Spirit.
1 Corinthians 12:3 NASB

Through times of trial and tribulation it can be easy to believe that God doesn't care or has abandoned you. But know that He is always there, just waiting to comfort you.

Lord, I know if I'm listening to a message that makes me depressed and defeated, that's from Satan. I know the one that says I'm worth dying for is from Christ.

Evening

Always There

Don't you know that you yourselves are God's temple and that God's Spirit dwells in your midst?
1 Corinthians 3:16 NIV

Although we can't physically touch God, we can feel His presence. He loves us, and when we ask Him to live in us, He gladly accepts the invitation. He has promised never to leave us, never to turn His back on us. And though He doesn't talk out loud to us, if we listen, we can hear Him speaking to us in our thoughts.

Dear Father, thank You for always being with me.

MORNING

A Healthy Fear

To fear the LORD is to hate evil;
I hate pride and arrogance, evil behavior and perverse speech.
PROVERBS 8:13 NIV

Our lives should reflect a similar reverence for our heavenly Father every day—our souls scrubbed extra clean, sin eliminated, and love for our Creator bursting forth in joy. God wants speech and actions to match. Take time today to stand in awe of the One who deserves our greatest respect and love.

Lord, help my daily actions and speech to reflect my respect for You. Amen.

EVENING

Simple Gossip

It is foolish to belittle one's neighbor; a sensible person keeps quiet.
A gossip goes around telling secrets, but those who
are trustworthy can keep a confidence.
PROVERBS 11:12–13 NLT

It's been said that if you have to glance at the door to see if anyone is coming before saying something, you probably shouldn't be saying it! This is a hard lesson to learn and an even harder action to put into practice, especially if all your friends do it, too.

Dear God, please forgive me when I have gossiped.
I know You want me to do—and say—the right thing.

DAY
256

MORNING

Peace, Be Still

GOD makes his people strong. GOD gives his people peace.
PSALM 29:11 MSG

At the center of life's storms, how do we find peace? If we're tossed about, struggling and hopeless, where is the peace? Don't worry—peace can be ours for the asking.

You see, *God* is our peace. He is ready to calm our storms when we call on Him. He will comfort and strengthen us each day.

Dear Lord, I thank You for Your protection.
Help me to keep my eyes on You. Please grant me peace.

EVENING

Fear Not

"Be strong and courageous. Do not be afraid or terrified because of them, for the LORD your God goes with you; he will never leave you nor forsake you."
DEUTERONOMY 31:6 NIV

Sometimes fear can stop you from doing the things you need to do and get in the way of the blessings God has for you. Being afraid to stand up for yourself, talk in front of a boardroom full of people, defend your beliefs, or reveal that hidden talent are fears that can keep you from fulfilling your destiny.

Dear God, I will not fear. I will trust
You to take care of me in every situation. Amen.

Morning

What's This Thing in My Eye?

"Why do you look at the speck of sawdust in your brother's eye and pay no attention to the plank in your own eye?"
Luke 6:41 NIV

In Luke 6:41, Jesus reminds us through His sawdust/plank analogy that none of us are blameless. It's important to put our own shortcomings into perspective when we face the temptation to judge others. Today, work on removing the plank from your eye and praise God for His gift of grace!

God, please help me to develop a gentle spirit that can share Your love and hope in a nonjudgmental way. Amen.

Evening

The Best Designer

How you made me is amazing and wonderful. I praise you for that. What you have done is wonderful. I know that very well.
Psalm 139:14 NIRV

Don't ever grumble or complain about how you look. You're more beautiful than a thousand dresses and created by a Designer who adores you. So hold your head high! Walk that runway and smile all the way. Celebrate your uniqueness and realize that your Designer is very, very pleased with how you've turned out.

God, I put my trust in Your design. Amen.

DAY 258

Morning

What Response Does God Require?

With what shall I come to the LORD and
bow myself before the God on high?
MICAH 6:6 NASB

Christ has already paid the price that needed to be exacted for our sins. The God of this universe looked upon our futility and became a man, and then He sacrificed His life so that we who did not and could not ever deserve His mercy might obtain it. Jesus Christ did all this because He is both just and kind.

Though I expend every effort, I can never rid myself of sin.
You've already provided the only way in which I can be cleansed.

Evening

Beautiful to Him

Let not yours be the [merely] external adorning with [elaborate] interweaving and knotting of the hair, the wearing of jewelry, or changes of clothes; but let it be the inward adorning and beauty of the hidden person of the heart, with the incorruptible and unfading charm of a gentle and peaceful spirit.
1 PETER 3:3–4 AMP

Who do you consider beautiful? Is that beauty only on the outside, or are you thinking of someone who shows inward beauty? Which do you focus on more for yourself? Do you need to adjust your focus a little bit?

Heavenly Father, thank You for seeing me as beautiful. Help me to focus less on outward beauty and more on becoming the godly woman You want me to be inside. Amen.

MORNING

My Way or God's Way?

*Good and upright is the LORD;
therefore He instructs sinners in the way.*
PSALM 25:8 NASB

God wants us to live life His way. Our good and upright God tells us that when we come before Him as humble, meek, needy, or afflicted, He will teach us what is right and just. God will teach us His way of living.

Good and upright God, please allow me not to be distracted in this world but to focus on You. Teach me Your way, I humbly pray. Amen.

EVENING

No One Understands Me

For this reason he had to be made like them, fully human in every way, in order that he might become a merciful and faithful high priest in service to God, and that he might make atonement for the sins of the people.
HEBREWS 2:17 NIV

Jesus gets you. And He wants a close relationship with you. He longs to be the One you turn to when no one else understands. He will never leave you hanging or fall short of what you need. He understands!

Thank You, Lord Jesus, for understanding me when I am not even sure I understand myself sometimes!

DAY 260

Morning

Choose Life

"The thief comes only to steal and kill and destroy;
I have come that they may have life, and have it to the full."
John 10:10 NIV

We have an enemy who delights in our believing such negative things, an enemy who wants only destruction for our souls. But Jesus came to give us life! We only have to choose it, as an act of the will blended with faith.

Loving Lord, help me daily to choose You and the life You want to give me. Give me the eyes of faith to trust that You will enable me to serve lovingly.

Evening

I Really Need That

Seek your happiness in the Lord,
and he will give you your heart's desire.
Psalm 37:4 GNT

If we give the desires of our hearts to the Lord, He can help us discover what is most important. He wants to be at the top of our wish list. We need Him first. And our relationship with Him is the key to happiness. After that, all the other things in our lives will come out in the right order of importance.

Dear Lord, I want to put You first on my list of wants.

Morning

Follow the Lord's Footsteps

"Come, follow me," Jesus said, "and I will send you out to fish for people."
Matthew 4:19 NIV

Following Jesus requires staying right on His heels. We need to be close enough to hear His whisper. Stay close to His heart by opening the Bible daily. Allow His Word to speak to your heart and give you direction. Throughout the day, offer up prayers for guidance and wisdom. Keep in step with Him, and His close presence will bless you beyond measure.

Dear Lord, grant me the desire to follow You.
Help me not to run ahead or lag behind. Amen.

Evening

Dream Big!

Now all glory to God, who is able, through his mighty power at work within us, to accomplish infinitely more than we might ask or think.
Ephesians 3:20 NLT

If things don't look so magnificent at the moment, you can rest assured that your heavenly Father is positioning you for bigger and better things to come.

God, I'm so excited that You have my customized future ready
and waiting. Help me stay on the path to Your best for me.
I know Your plans are the best plans. Amen.

DAY
262

MORNING

How to Know If You're in Love

If I speak with the tongues of men and of angels, but do not have love, I have become a noisy gong or a clanging cymbal.
1 CORINTHIANS 13:1 NASB

To truly love someone means that we will always place that person's welfare above our own. This, after all, is how God loves us.

Lord, help me exhibit true love.

EVENING

God Is Always Awake

My help comes from the LORD, who made heaven and earth! He will not let you stumble; the one who watches over you will not slumber. Indeed, he who watches over Israel never slumbers or sleeps. The LORD himself watches over you!
PSALM 121:2–5 NLT

God gives you His peace, which will actually guard your heart and your mind (Philippians 4:6–7)! We can't even understand how that happens, but it really does. Give it a try, and give your worries to God. He's always awake.

God, thanks for not being bored by my problems. Show me Your peace.

Morning

Budget Breaker

Then the Lord *said to Moses, "Behold, I will rain bread from heaven for you; and the people shall go out and gather a day's portion every day, that I may test them, whether or not they will walk in My instruction."*
Exodus 16:4 NASB

God is faithful in spite of us! He will meet our needs when we come to Him in simple trust. Then we can bask in His faithfulness.

Father, Your Word promises to supply all my needs. I trust You in spite of the challenges I see. You are ever faithful. Thank You!

Evening

Joy in Trusting God

But let all those rejoice who put their trust in You; let them ever shout for joy, because You defend them; let those also who love Your name be joyful in You.
Psalm 5:11 NKJV

Do you ever find that you've put your trust in the wrong things? That you've trusted your friends more than God? Have you felt you've gone in the wrong direction because you weren't fully trusting God? Put your full trust in Him, and feel the joy!

Dear God, please help me to trust in You to guide me in the decisions I need to make each day.

DAY
264

Morning

Annual or Perennial?

They are like trees planted along the riverbank, bearing fruit each season.
Their leaves never wither, and they prosper in all they do.
Psalm 1:3 NLT

First, be a perennial—long lasting, enduring, slow growing, steady, and faithful. Second, don't be discouraged by your inevitable dormant seasons. Tend to your soul, and it will reward you with years of lush blossoms.

Father, be the gardener of my soul. Amen.

Evening

Rescue Squad

The Lord *says, "I will rescue those who love me.*
I will protect those who trust in my name."
Psalm 91:14 NLT

God saves us from sin. Sin carries the promise of eternal devastation—far worse than anything we could experience here on this earth. God offers the blood of Jesus as our rescue from sin.

Dear God, please forgive me for my sin and rescue me with the gift of eternal life. I want to walk with You. I'd love it if You'd protect me from danger in this life, too. Amen.

Morning

Have You Looked Up?

The heavens proclaim the glory of God.
The skies display his craftsmanship.
Psalm 19:1 NLT

God has placed glimpses of creation's majesty—evidence of His love—throughout our world. But we must develop eyes to see these reminders in our daily life and not let the cares and busyness of our lives keep our heads turned down.

Have you looked up today?

Lord, open my eyes! Unstuff my ears! Teach me to see the wonders of Your creation every day and to point them out to my children.

Evening

When the Going Gets Tough. . .

The Lord is my strength and my shield; my heart trusts in Him, and I am helped; therefore my heart exults, and with my song I shall thank Him.
Psalm 28:7 NASB

What does it mean to trust God? You lay down your "own understanding" and "acknowledge" that He has always been, is, and always will be the supreme God of all creation (Proverbs 3:5–6).

I trust You, Lord God. Please give me the strength to "press on toward the goal for the prize" (Philippians 3:14 NASB). In Jesus' precious and holy name, I pray. Amen.

DAY 266

MORNING

True Environmentalists

"But now ask the beasts, and let them teach you;
and the birds of the heavens, and let them tell you."
JOB 12:7 NASB

"For in Him all things were created, both in the heavens and on earth. . . all things have been created through Him and for Him" (Colossians 1:16 NASB). It's important to remember that Christ created animals for our enjoyment. Therefore, be grateful to the Lord.

Lord, I know that even if I didn't have Your written Word,
the order and perfection of Your creation still prove Your existence!

EVENING

Tick, Tick, Tick

These are evil times, so make every minute count.
EPHESIANS 5:16 CEV

Ask God to remind you when it's time to turn off your gadgets and do something more worthwhile. Remember that He has great plans for your life, and He wants you to get started on them!

Father in heaven, I don't want to neglect Your Word. Help me to be careful with the time I spend online, and tap on my shoulder if I start to get careless. Amen.

Morning

Water's Cost

"To the thirsty I will give water without cost from the spring of the water of life."
Revelation 21:6 NIV

Just as we cannot live without water, we cannot live without the Word of God. Jesus loves us so much that He gave up His life that we might partake of these invigorating waters. So drink up, and leave your money at home; the water of life is free.

Dear Lord, thank You for letting me drink for free from the spring of the water of life. Help me to remember Your sacrifice and Your love for me. Amen.

Evening

Marsupials in the Dark

"Never will I leave you; never will I forsake you."
Hebrews 13:5 NIV

God can see you all the time. When you feel like you are walking in the dark and feel like God isn't with you, remember He is always with you.

Lord Jesus, thank You that You say You will never leave me nor forsake me. And even though I don't always feel like You are with me, I trust that You are because You say You are. I lean on what You say, not on how I feel. Amen.

DAY
268

Morning

You Are an Answer to Prayer

He comforts us when we are in trouble,
so that we can share that same comfort with others in trouble.
2 Corinthians 1:4 cev

It can be difficult to move past that point of being ministered to, in order to minister to others in need. But, according to the apostle Paul, one of the reasons God comforts us is so we can share that comfort with others when they need it.

So when someone is praying for comfort, be ready—it might just be you whom God will send to minister to that hurting soul.

Jesus, please help me open my heart
and eyes to see the needs around me.

Evening

Let Go!

The other guests began to say among themselves,
"Who is this who even forgives sins?"
Luke 7:49 niv

The good news is that God forgives you. He knows your heart. All you need to do is ask, and He will forgive any wrong you've done. He forgives everything from the smallest mistakes to the biggest blunders.

God, please help me to learn to forgive
myself as You have forgiven me.

MORNING

Faultless

To him who is able to keep you from stumbling and to present you before his glorious presence without fault and with great joy.
JUDE 1:24 NIV

Jesus is the One who can keep us from stumbling—who can present us faultless before the Father. Whether we have done wrong and denied it or have been falsely accused, we can come into His presence to be restored and lifted up. Let us keep our eyes on Him instead of on our need to justify ourselves to God or others.

Thank You, Jesus, for Your cleansing love and for the joy we can find in Your presence. Amen.

EVENING

The Great Blue Ocean

Because of the LORD's great love we are not consumed, for his compassions never fail. They are new every morning; great is your faithfulness.
LAMENTATIONS 3:22–23 NIV

His kindness will never fail. It's new every morning like the dew on your lawn and the rising of the sun. God's love is sure, and His faithfulness is forever.

Even when I'm not very faithful to You, Lord, and I sometimes forget to talk to You, I'm glad You love me and watch over me. Thank You for Your love and faithfulness that is as wide and deep as the great blue ocean. Amen.

DAY
270

Morning

Reflecting God in Our Work

*Whatever you do, work at it with all your heart,
as working for the Lord, not for human masters.*
COLOSSIANS 3:23 NIV

Our attitudes and actions on the job speak volumes to those around us. Although it may be tempting to do just enough to get by, we put forth our best effort when we remember we represent God to the world. A Christian's character on the job should be a positive reflection of the Lord.

*Father, help me today to represent You well through my work.
I want to reflect Your love in all I do. Amen.*

Evening

Promises, Promises

"God is not human, that he should lie, not a human being, that he should change his mind. Does he speak and then not act? Does he promise and not fulfill?"
NUMBERS 23:19 NIV

God always, *always* keeps His promises. He's not like human beings, who forget or mess up or who can't control their circumstances. If God says He'll do something, He means it. And He'll do it!

*Dear Father, thank You for keeping Your promises. Help me
to learn more about Your promises through Your Word. Amen.*

Morning

Whom Do You Follow?

*For every house is built by someone,
but the builder of all things is God.*
Hebrews 3:4 NASB

The writer of the book of Hebrews speaks with conviction and understanding. "Encourage one another day after day, as long as it is still called 'Today,' so that none of you will be hardened by the deceitfulness of sin. For we have become partakers of Christ, if we hold fast the beginning of our assurance firm until the end" (Hebrews 3:13–14 NASB).

Man's memory of his own disobedience is so quickly forgotten, Lord. The opportunity to follow Christ lies before me. Lord, help me to respond.

Evening

Heartbreak Hotel

*The Lord is close to the brokenhearted
and saves those who are crushed in spirit.*
Psalm 34:18 NIV

In some people a broken heart can lead to bitterness, anger, and depression. But you don't have to go there. You're a child of God. He sees everything, and He knows just how you feel. You can choose to turn all that hurt over to Him.

Dear God, I ask You to heal my broken heart today. Help me release all my hurts to You so that I can live a life of joy and freedom. Amen.

DAY
272

Morning

Do Not Be Afraid

"Do not be afraid, for I have ransomed you.
I have called you by name; you are mine."
Isaiah 43:1 NLT

But in the midst of all trouble, Jesus walks beside us. He holds our noses above the water; He wraps us in flame-retardant clothing. We will not drown, nor will we be consumed in the fiery furnace. Why? Because He ransomed us. He paid sin's penalty, He delivered us from the slave market of sin, and He calls us by name.

Lord, I am Yours, and You will enable me to
walk through the dangers that surround me.

Evening

Fully Understood

This High Priest of ours understands our weaknesses,
for he faced all of the same testings we do, yet he did not sin.
Hebrews 4:15 NLT

Jesus Christ understands everything about every one of His creations. He knows how you feel on the best of your best days and on the worst of your worst days. And usually it's hardest to find someone who understands us in the difficult times. He knows what it's like not to be understood, but He truly understands all about us. Trust that He "gets it."

Dear Jesus, thank You for understanding
everything about me and loving me anyway.

MORNING

Forgiven Much

She began to wet his feet with her tears. Then she wiped them with her hair, kissed them and poured perfume on them.
LUKE 7:38 NIV

Extravagant forgiveness and extravagant love were displayed the day that the woman of ill repute washed Jesus' feet. Christ told her to go in peace. Another life changed by the Master.

Lord, teach me to love You more.
I have been forgiven much. Amen.

EVENING

More Than Ordinary

"And I tell you that you are Peter, and on this rock I will build my church, and the gates of Hades will not overcome it."
MATTHEW 16:18 NIV

Know this: if you're feeling very ordinary, then you're the perfect person to do extraordinary things!

God, help me to see myself as You see me—
capable of extraordinary things. Amen.

DAY
274

MORNING

Just Half a Cup

"I am coming to you now, but I say these things while I am still in the world, so that they may have the full measure of my joy within them."
JOHN 17:13 NIV

Our Father longs to bestow His richest blessings and wisdom on us. He loves us, so He desires to fill our cup to overflowing with the things that He knows will bring us pleasure and growth.

Dear Jesus, forgive me for not accepting the fullness of Your blessings and Your joy. Help me to see the ways that I prevent my cup from being filled to overflowing.

EVENING

Immeasurable Rewards

Blessed is the one who perseveres under trial because, having stood the test, that person will receive the crown of life that the Lord has promised to those who love him.
JAMES 1:12 NIV

The Bible reminds us that this life is going to be hard. We're going to have lots of temptations and lots of trials. But by making the right choices—following God's guidelines for our lives—the rewards will be immeasurable.

God, help me to guard my mind and my heart so that I can do the right thing today. Amen.

Morning

Hide and Seek

"And do you seek great things for yourself? Seek them not, for behold, I am bringing disaster upon all flesh, declares the LORD."
JEREMIAH 45:5 ESV

Jesus tells us what we should seek: the kingdom of God and His righteousness (Matthew 6:33). He won't hide from us. When we seek the right things, He'll give us every good and perfect gift (James 1:17). And that will be more than we can ask or dream.

Lord, please teach me to seek not greatness, but You. May You be the all in all of my life.

Evening

Don't Be Afraid

When I am afraid, I put my trust in you.
PSALM 56:3 NIV

In Luke 12:32, after telling us how useless it is to worry, Jesus says, "Do not be afraid, little flock, for your Father has been pleased to give you the kingdom" (NIV). Can't you hear and feel the love in God's heart for you? When you are afraid, give it to Jesus.

Dear God, when I'm afraid, please help me to remember that You are always with me and that I can talk to You about it. Please give me Your peace.

DAY
276

Morning

For What Are You Zealous?

For am I now seeking the favor of men, or of God? Or am I striving to please men? If I were still trying to please men, I would not be a bond-servant of Christ.
Galatians 1:10 NASB

Paul didn't sit around asking men for their opinions. Christ's call was sufficient. Therefore, he devoted himself to study, prayer, and meditation alone with his Lord. For although he'd known the scriptures, he had approached them from the wrong perspective.

Lord, what are my own misconceptions concerning Your Word? Teach me the true meaning of the scriptures.

Evening

A Real Happily Ever After

Whoever believes in the Son has eternal life.
John 3:36 NRSV

Don't you just love a happy ending? God does! That's why He has the perfect happily ever after planned out for you. It's all going to take place in a land far, far away. . .a place called heaven. In that regal place, you'll walk on streets of gold, live in a mansion, and dine with the King! It's true!

God, I believe You sent Your Son, Jesus, to die for my sins. Thank You, Lord! Amen.

MORNING

Location, Location, Location

This I declare about the LORD: he alone is my refuge, my place of safety; he is my God, and I trust him.
PSALM 91:2 NLT

If you are abiding in Christ, moment by moment, you are constantly safe under His protection. In that secret place, that hidden place in Him, you can maintain a holy serenity, a peace of mind that surpasses all understanding. If you are trusting in God, nothing can move you or harm you.

God, You are my refuge. Fill me with Your light and the peace of Your love. It's You and me, Lord, all the way! Amen.

EVENING

God "Gets" You

O LORD, you have searched me and known me! You know when I sit down and when I rise up; you discern my thoughts from afar.
PSALM 139:1–2 ESV

God knows you! He understands your quirks and sense of humor because He gave them to you. He understands your mood swings, worries, and dreams. And He knows what you've struggled with in the past and what you struggle with today. He has compassion and wants to help you. All you have to do is cry out to Him, and He will listen.

God, thank You for listening to me and understanding me.

MORNING

An Hour Apart

And he cometh unto the disciples, and findeth them asleep, and saith unto Peter, What, could ye not watch with me one hour?
MATTHEW 26:40 KJV

Ask God to make you a doer of His Word, not only a hearer. Then, as a final step, share what God has taught you with someone else.

Lord and Savior, show me when and how to carve out an hour with You. Make me hungry for that intimate time.

EVENING

God Is in Control

In peace I will lie down and sleep, for you alone, O LORD, will keep me safe.
PSALM 4:8 NLT

The Bible promises that one day there will be no more tears and no more trials. In heaven there will be no scary news reports and there will be no more pain. Until then, rest in the knowledge that God has commanded angels to watch over you. Lay your head on your pillow at night in peace. God is your safety. Nothing can reach you that hasn't first been filtered through His fingers.

God, I trust that You are in control. Amen.

Morning

Truth in Love

O Lord, correct me, but with justice; not in Your anger,
lest You bring me to nothing.
Jeremiah 10:24 NKJV

Our tendency is to rationalize our sinful behavior. Thankfully, God has given us the gift of the Holy Spirit to help us on our journey. If we ask, the Lord is faithful to His Word and He will reveal our motivations to us.

Thank You, Father, that You are the discerner of hearts, that You gently show me my sin, and that You have given me Your Holy Spirit to help me.

Evening

I Love That!

But God, being rich in mercy, because of His great love with which He loved us, even when we were dead in our transgressions, made us alive together with Christ.
Ephesians 2:4–5 NASB

The only way is to know who lives behind the word *love*: God *is* love. God loves us with something deeper than a word. He loves us with His entire being, as our Father and Creator. And it's a *big* love! Only when we know more of Him can we understand what His love really means.

Thank You, God, for Your great love for me.

Morning

Get Those Hammers Ready

Now therefore, thus says the LORD of hosts, "Consider your ways!"
HAGGAI 1:5 NASB

God commissioned Haggai to bring His motivating Word to the people.

The task loomed larger than life, so the Lord spoke again: " 'Take courage,' declares the LORD, 'and work; for I am with you' " (Haggai 2:4 NASB).

Lord, whatever task is overwhelming me today
You have the strength to see it through to fulfillment.

Evening

Do I Need It or Want It?

Not that we are sufficient of ourselves to think of anything
as being from ourselves, but our sufficiency is from God.
2 CORINTHIANS 3:5 NKJV

God supplies our needs through our jobs, family, and community. There are times when our heavenly Father is more than happy to give you the things you want, but His primary job is caring for your everyday needs so you can live out the purpose He has for you!

Dear God, help me to recognize the difference between the wants
and needs in my life. Thank You for always supplying my needs. Amen.

Morning

Light My Path

Your word is a lamp for my feet, a light on my path.
Psalm 119:105 NIV

When we sincerely begin to search God's Word, we find the path becomes clear. We see everything in a new light, a light that makes it obvious which way to turn and what choices to make. God's light allows us to live our lives in the most fulfilling way possible, a way planned out from the very beginning by God Himself.

Jesus, shine Your light upon my path. I have spent too long wandering through the darkness, looking for my way.

Evening

Me, Beautiful?

God hasn't invited us into a disorderly, unkempt life but into something holy and beautiful—as beautiful on the inside as the outside.
1 Thessalonians 4:7 MSG

God loves you just as you are. Strive to live each day the way He would have you live it. Be kind to others and think of them more than of what you look like.

Dear God, please help me to be more concerned with others and doing Your will than I am with the way I look.

DAY
282

Morning

A Different Cup to Fill

O God, thou art my God; early will I seek thee.
PSALM 63:1 KJV

If the king of Israel recognized his need to spend time with God, how much more should we? When we seek our heavenly Father before daily activities demand our attention, the Holy Spirit regenerates our spirits, and our cups overflow.

Dear Lord, I take this time to pray and spend time with You before I attend to daily responsibilities. Give me the wisdom and direction I need today. Amen.

Evening

The Hope of His Calling

I pray that the eyes of your heart may be enlightened,
so that you will know what is the hope of His calling.
EPHESIANS 1:18 NASB

God's Word is our guidebook—our life manual. Everything we need to know about how God has called us to live is inside, waiting to be discovered! It is by *knowing* His hopeful calling and His Word that you will blossom into the woman He has called you to be.

Lord, I know that I am and always will be Yours—
and for that I have eternal hope!

Morning

Power Up

The Spirit of God, who raised Jesus from the dead, lives in you.
Romans 8:11 NLT

We don't have to go it alone. Our heavenly Father wants to help. All we have to do is ask. He has already made His power available to His children. Whatever we face—wherever we go—whatever dreams we have for our lives, take courage and know that anything is possible when we draw on the power of God.

Father, help me to remember that You are always with me, ready to help me do all things. Amen.

Evening

Hope: An Anchor for the Soul

Be strong and take heart, all you who hope in the Lord.
Psalm 31:24 NIV

Just as an anchor holds a boat steady when the waves are rolling, God's hope holds your thoughts and your emotions steady when life is difficult. All you have to do is believe and trust God. Then you can be steady even in a big storm of life.

Lord Jesus, I am glad that You are always my anchor and that You will never leave me.

DAY
284

Morning

Comfort Food

For whatever things were written before were written for our learning, that we through the patience and comfort of the Scriptures might have hope.
Romans 15:4 NKJV

The words of God are soothing and provide permanent hope and peace. Through God's Word, you will be changed, and your troubles will dim in the bright light of Christ. So the next time you are sad, lonely, or disappointed, turn to the Word of God as your source of comfort.

Father, help me to remember to find my comfort in scripture rather than through earthly things that will ultimately fail me. Amen.

Evening

Worry Doesn't Help

Jesus said, "That is why I tell you not to worry about everyday life—whether you have enough food to eat or enough clothes to wear."
Luke 12:22 NLT

Jesus doesn't want you to worry about having the best clothes or the most expensive hairstyle. You don't have to be afraid of what's going to happen to you in this future or who will come and go in your life. The Bible says that worry won't change a thing, so trust God instead.

Dear God, forgive me for all the times I worry. I want to trust that You're in control. Please give me Your peace.

Morning

The Fruit of the Spirit

But the fruit of the Spirit is love, joy, peace, patience, kindness, goodness, faithfulness, gentleness, self-control; against such things there is no law. . . . If we live by the Spirit, let us also walk by the Spirit.
GALATIANS 5:22–23, 25 NASB

Why is God showering us with these gifts? Because they prove that He can enter a human life and affect her or him with change, that others might also be won to Christ as they observe this miracle.

Lord, my greatest gift from You is salvation; Your grace enables me to begin life with a fresh start and show others your goodness.

Evening

Your Best Interests

"And he is not served by human hands, as if he needed anything. Rather, he himself gives everyone life and breath and everything else."
ACTS 17:25 NIV

Sometimes God gives you just what you need. Remember, He always has your best interests at heart.

Lord, I really do appreciate having new things. I don't want to be selfish. Help me to understand that wants and needs are two different things. Please show me how to be content with what I have. Amen.

DAY
286

Morning

Creating Margin

"My Presence will go with you, and I will give you rest."
Exodus 33:14 NIV

God believes in rest! But most of us live lives that are packed to the brim with activities and obligations. We're overwhelmed. With such a fragile balance, unexpected occurrences, like a dead car battery, can wreck us emotionally, spiritually, and physically.

Life is busy. But in God's presence we find rest.

Help me, Father, to listen to Your instruction and heed Your words, that I might find much-needed rest.

Evening

A Plan for Me?

"I know what I'm doing. I have it all planned out—plans to take care of you, not abandon you, plans to give you the future you hope for."
Jeremiah 29:11 MSG

Trust in God's wisdom and know that He really does care for you and wants the very best for you. Knowing that's true and knowing that He sees all things, does that make it easier for you to let go of your own will and trust Him fully?

Father, I give up my own will and surrender control to You.

Morning

Power of the Word

*"The Spirit gives life; the flesh counts for nothing.
The words I have spoken to you—
they are full of the Spirit and life."*
John 6:63 NIV

If the Word is in our mind or before our eyes and ears, the Holy Spirit can work it into our hearts and our consciences. Jesus told us to abide in His Word. That's our part, putting ourselves in a place to hear and receive the Word. The rest is the beautiful and mysterious work of the Spirit.

Thank You, Jesus, the Living Word, who changes my heart and my mind through the power of Your Word.

Evening

Pretty Special

*"Fear not, for I have redeemed you.
I have called you by name, you are mine."*
Isaiah 43:1 ESV

The reason God loves us so much is because we are important to Him. Next time you feel forgotten, or like you don't matter, remind yourself of this one truth: *The God of the universe, the King of kings and Lord of lords, calls me by name. That makes me pretty special!*

Dear Father, help me to remember who I am in You. Help me make others feel special, too.

DAY
288

MORNING

Nothing to Lose

Saul replied, "You are not able to go out against this Philistine and fight him; you are only a young man, and he has been a warrior from his youth."
1 SAMUEL 17:33 NIV

If God is fighting your battle for you, trust in Him, seek godly counsel, and follow His call implicitly. You have nothing to lose.

If You lead me, Lord, I cannot lose.
Show me Your path and give me courage. Amen.

EVENING

Your Smile Makes God Smile!

Charm is deceptive, and beauty does not last;
but a woman who fears the LORD will be greatly praised.
PROVERBS 31:30 NLT

A truly beautiful person shines from the inside out. So give everyone a great big smile! Your beauty comes from the inside out. A great smile brightens everyone's day and warms the heart of God. And making God smile is all that really matters.

God, help my beauty to come from inside and let
my smile make someone else happy today, too. Amen.

Morning

Taking a Real Sabbath

By the seventh day God had finished the work he had been doing; so on the seventh day he rested from all his work.
Genesis 2:2 NIV

God created the Sabbath. He did it not so we could have another commandment to keep, but for our own good. Our bodies, minds, and emotions need rest. The Sabbath gives us a chance to take a breather. As we slow down our schedule and quiet our hearts, we can more easily hear from Him.

God, forgive me for taking Your commands too lightly. Help me to remember the Sabbath and keep it holy, just as You did.

Evening

Rainbow Girl

O lord, thou hast searched me, and known me.
Psalm 139:1 KJV

Tell your Creator! He understands you like no one can and knows exactly how to brighten a dark, unbecoming mood. Pray about your feelings. Remember that as God's girl, you have the power to rule over them instead of letting them rule you!

Dear God my Creator, You know how I feel and why. Teach me to control my feelings before they cause me to act in an unbecoming way. Amen.

DAY
290

Morning

Chosen before the Foundation of the World

Blessed be the God and Father of our Lord Jesus Christ, who has blessed us with every spiritual blessing in the heavenly places in Christ.
Ephesians 1:3 NASB

When God created the world, He not only planned your place in it, but He also reserved a place in heaven for you. Now, you can either claim your ticket by accepting Christ's salvation on your behalf, or you can cancel the reservation by never responding to God's offer.

Lord, help me and each woman reading this to enjoy the safety, protection, and sense of belonging that come from being chosen.

Evening

It's Tough to Lose Someone You Love

We believe that God will bring with Jesus those who have fallen asleep in him.
1 Thessalonians 4:14 NIV

Because you are a believer, death has no hold on you (1 Corinthians 15:55). When Jesus died and rose again, He defeated death once and for all. The Bible says that when believers leave this life, they go to be with the Lord (2 Corinthians 5:8).

Dear God, thank You for defeating death for me and those I love. Amen.

Morning

Lost and Found

"And the one who sent me is with me—he has not deserted me.
For I always do what pleases him."
John 8:29 NLT

The further we displace ourselves from God—not necessarily on purpose—the more we become lost in our own space. If you feel distant from Him today, look up. He's waiting for you to find your rightful place with Him.

God, show me what things I should commit to and what things
are for someone else to do, so that I am available to You
and ready to serve in the capacity
You've prepared me for. Amen.

Evening

Choosing the Right Thing

And whatever you do [no matter what it is] in word or deed,
do everything in the name of the Lord Jesus and in [dependence upon]
His Person, giving praise to God the Father through Him.
Colossians 3:17 AMP

All decisions—large or small—should be made in order to bring our heavenly Father the praise He deserves.

Dear Father, help me to seek Your guidance as I make decisions.

DAY 292

MORNING

Pick Your Battles

To these four young men God gave knowledge and understanding of all kinds of literature and learning. And Daniel could understand visions and dreams of all kinds.
DANIEL 1:17 NIV

Surprisingly, God didn't tackle every single issue in Babylon. He picked Daniel's battles for him, and Daniel was greatly used in the midst of a pagan culture. Not indignant or antagonistic, but compassionate and seeking the best for his captors.

Can we be Daniels in our communities today?

Lord, show me how to seek Your wisdom and discernment while picking my battles. Help me to love those who oppose You.

EVENING

The King, My Protector

Neither death nor life, neither angels nor demons, neither the present nor the future, nor any powers, neither height nor depth, nor anything else in all creation, will be able to separate us from the love of God that is in Christ Jesus our Lord.
ROMANS 8:38–39 NIV

You can have confidence that nothing in this world can keep you from God. Nothing in this world can separate you from God. And nothing—absolutely nothing—can take away your eternal life in Him. Your future—your eternity—is protected.

God, thank You that nothing can separate me from Your love.

MORNING

My Helper

So we say with confidence, "The Lord is my helper;
I will not be afraid. What can mere mortals do to me?"
HEBREWS 13:6 NIV

When you're up against a tough situation, your heavenly Father is standing right there, speaking positive words over you, telling you that you have what it takes to be the best you can possibly be. And while He won't take the reins—He wants you to learn from the experience, after all—He will advise you as you go.

Father, You're the best helper possible. Thank You for
taking my fears and replacing them with godly confidence.

EVENING

Secret Service Man

Deliver me from my enemies, O my God;
protect me from those who rise up against me.
PSALM 59:1 NRSV

God is always on your side, protecting you from the enemy. You don't always see how He protects you, but He does! He keeps you safe. He protects you from harm as you sleep at night. He sends His angels to watch over you and guards your steps everywhere you go. Why? Because He loves you. You're his daughter, after all!

Thank You, Lord, for protecting me!

DAY
294

Morning

Can God Interrupt You?

In their hearts humans plan their course,
but the Lord establishes their steps.
Proverbs 16:9 NIV

God sees the big picture. Be open. Be flexible. Allow God to change your plans in order to accomplish His divine purposes. Instead of becoming frustrated, look for ways the Lord might be working. Be willing to join Him. When we do, interruptions become blessings.

Dear Lord, forgive me when I am so rigidly locked into my own agenda that I miss Yours. Give me Your eternal perspective so that I may be open to divine interruptions. Amen.

Evening

You've Got Talent!

He will never give up on you. Never forget that.
1 Corinthians 1:9 MSG

If we hide our talents, we're no better than the servant who buried his talent. (And God called him wicked!) Don't let fear or laziness keep you from shining for God. Remember, God gave you those talents, and He will gladly help you develop them and use them for His purposes.

Thank You, God, for giving me special talents unique to me. Amen.

MORNING

The Meaning of True Christian Fellowship

I thank my God in all my remembrance of you,
always offering prayer with joy in my every prayer for you all.
PHILIPPIANS 1:3–4 NASB

Paul's joy is not dependent on circumstances. Rather, it overflows from the content of his heart, where the true source of joy resides, Jesus Christ. And because of this indwelling, Paul senses a oneness with other believers, despite the fact that they are far from him. It is the love of Christ that binds them together.

Lord, might I pray as Paul: "I press on toward the goal for the prize of the upward call of God in Christ Jesus" (Philippians 3:14 NASB).

EVENING

A Grand Adventure

"For I know the plans I have for you," declares the LORD,
"plans to prosper you and not to harm you, plans to give you hope and a future."
JEREMIAH 29:11 NIV

God has a design for your whole life, just like a beautiful picture. He wants the best for you—a one-of-a-kind, grand adventure—better than you could ever imagine for yourself. He wants to help you make the most of your talents and keep you close to Him.

Thank You, God, that You have a perfect design for my life.

DAY
296

Morning

Trouble or Trust?

"Don't let your hearts be troubled.
Trust in God, and trust also in me."
John 14:1 NLT

You do not know what your future holds, but Christ does. He asks you to stop worrying. He asks you to trust in Him. He is faithful to provide for His own.

Lord, please replace trouble with trust in this heart of mine that is sometimes lonely and unsure of the future. Thank You, Jesus, that I can trust in You. Amen.

Evening

Promise Keeper

"I have set my rainbow in the clouds, and it will
be the sign of the covenant between me and the earth."
Genesis 9:13 NIV

God keeps His promises. You can rest assured He will never again flood the whole earth as He did in Noah's day. And if He keeps that promise, wouldn't it make sense that our God would keep all of His promises?

Heavenly Father, thank You for the rainbow in the sky
that reminds me I serve a promise-keeping God! Amen.

Morning

Marvelous Thunder

*"God's voice thunders in marvelous ways;
he does great things beyond our understanding."*
Job 37:5 NIV

The One who controls nature also holds every one of our tears in His hand. He is our Father, and He works on our behalf. He is more than enough to meet our needs; He does things far beyond what our human minds can understand.

Lord God, You are power. You hold all things in Your hand and You chose to love me. Please help me trust in Your power, never my own.

Evening

The Force of the Flow

"Be strong and courageous. Do not be afraid or terrified because of them, for the Lord *your God goes with you; he will never leave you nor forsake you."*
Deuteronomy 31:6 NIV

By eliminating fear within, knowing you are not alone, and recognizing He is there to show you the way to success, you cause your courage level to hit maximum flow!

*God, help me to be brave and strong.
I know You are with me through everything. Amen.*

DAY
298

MORNING

Eye Care

For thus says the LORD of hosts. . .
"He who touches you touches the apple of His eye."
ZECHARIAH 2:8 NKJV

When something or someone attacks us, God feels our pain. He is instantly aware of our discomfort, for it is His own. When the storms of life come, we must remember how God feels each twinge of suffering. Despite the adversity, we can praise God, for He is sheltering us.

Thank You, God, that You are so aware of what is happening to me.
Thank You for Your protection. Amen.

EVENING

Christ's Ambassadors

For God was in Christ, reconciling the world to himself,
no longer counting people's sins against them.
2 CORINTHIANS 5:19 NLT

It's a very important job to tell—and show—others about what God has done in our lives. Because of the great love that Jesus showed for us on the cross, God is not counting our sins against us! We're free from guilt! Free from shame! And free to live a life of joy for all eternity!

Dear Jesus, thank You for not counting my sins against me.
Thank You for Your great love.

Morning

Born Again to a Living Hope

In this you greatly rejoice, even though now for a little while, if necessary, you have been distressed by various trials, so that the proof of your faith, being more precious than gold which is perishable, even though tested by fire, may be found to result in praise and glory and honor at the revelation of Jesus Christ.
1 Peter 1:6–7 NASB

When the multitude became divided as to Christ's true identity and many wanted to seize Jesus, Nicodemus, who could no longer remain silent, reminded them that their law couldn't judge a man without a proper hearing (John 7:51).

Thank You, Jesus, for convicting my soul today, and for strengthening my faith as I grow into a person who glorifies Christ each day.

Evening

How Can I Make Someone Love Me?

We love because he first loved us.
1 John 4:19 NIV

This is wonderful because it means that you don't have to be perfect or beautiful, rich or smart to get true love. This is how God loves. He loves us even though we aren't perfect. Even if you are stubborn, mean, impatient, or unkind, God will never stop loving you.

Lord, I am so thankful that there is nothing I need to do to earn Your love.

MORNING

God's Mountain Sanctuary

*And seeing the multitudes, he went up into a mountain: and. . .
his disciples came unto him: and he opened his mouth, and taught them.*
MATTHEW 5:1–2 KJV

Do you yearn for a place where problems evaporate like the morning dew? Do you need a place of solace? God is wherever you are—behind a bedroom door, nestled alongside you in your favorite chair, or even standing at a sink full of dirty dishes. Come apart and enter God's mountain sanctuary.

Heavenly Father, help me to find sanctuary in Your abiding presence. Amen.

EVENING

I Have All I Need

*Just think—you don't need a thing, you've got it all!
All God's gifts are right in front of you as you wait expectantly
for our Master Jesus to arrive on the scene for the Finale.*
1 CORINTHIANS 1:7 MSG

When you think you just have to have a new designer dress, purse, or shoes and others say you don't need them, maybe it's time to reflect on your true needs and realize that God has provided all you really need and then some.

*Dear God, help me to realize that I already
have everything I could possibly need! Amen.*

MORNING

More Than Enough

Let us not become weary in doing good, for at the proper time we will reap a harvest if we do not give up.
GALATIANS 6:9 NIV

We can only imagine what that harvest might be, because we know that God is the God of "immeasurably more than all we ask or imagine" (Ephesians 3:20 NIV). We can be recipients of His "immeasurably more" if we press on in the strength He provides.

Father, fill me with Your strength so I can carry on. I long to reap the harvest You have for me.

EVENING

The Seedling Principle

"Truly, truly, I say to you, unless a grain of wheat falls into the earth and dies, it remains alone; but if it dies, it bears much fruit."
JOHN 12:24 NASB

Just remember, God has given you everything you *need*: His everlasting love.

Lord, I trust You. Help me to die to myself and grow in You. The desire of my heart is to follow You no matter what. Please help me to walk with You and not let go. In Jesus' name I pray. Amen.

DAY
302

Morning

A Woman's Work

Well reported of for good works; if she have brought up children, if she have lodged strangers, if she have washed the saints' feet, if she have relieved the afflicted, if she have diligently followed every good work.
1 Timothy 5:10 KJV

This is the humble work God honors, the work that will one day be praised.

Dear Lord, Your Word is so clear on what You expect of me. How can I miss it? And why do I so easily reject it? Teach me contentment in my calling as a woman, knowing that You will reward the humble labor of homemaking. Amen.

Evening

What a Glorious Day!

"And everyone who has left houses or brothers or sisters or father or mother or wife or children or fields for my sake will receive a hundred times as much and will inherit eternal life."
Matthew 19:29 NIV

God reminds you that He offers the gift of eternal life—and you've already accepted that wonderful gift. Someday your loved ones will greet you in heaven. What a glorious day that will be!

God, thank You for offering me eternal life. Take care of my loved ones until I get to heaven. Amen.

Morning

A Fragrant Offering

Follow God's example, therefore, as dearly loved children and walk in the way of love, just as Christ loved us and gave himself up for us as a fragrant offering and sacrifice to God.
Ephesians 5:1–2 NIV

As we live a life of love in front of those we care for, we exude the sweetest fragrance of all—Christ. That's one aroma that can't be bottled!

Dear Lord, I long to live a life that points people to You. As I care for those in need, may the sweet-smelling aroma of You and Your love be an invitation for people to draw near.

Evening

I Can Do It!

"This is my command—be strong and courageous! Do not be afraid or discouraged. For the Lord your God is with you wherever you go."
Joshua 1:9 NLT

God will provide all the courage you need if only you will believe. He will go with you into every scary situation. When you feel discouraged, remember how big God is compared to whatever it is you have to accomplish. With God, you can do anything—even slay giants!

Heavenly Father, help me to see that nothing—not even a giant—is too big for You. Amen.

DAY
304

MORNING

The Promise Remains

Therefore, let us fear if, while a promise remains of entering His rest, any one of you may seem to have come short of it. For indeed we have had good news preached to us, just as they also; but the word they heard did not profit them, because it was not united by faith in those who heard.
HEBREWS 4:1–2 NASB

Today's scripture is about "entering into God's rest," something that those who do not choose Him will never experience.

Dear God, I know You have kept Your part of the bargain, in obtaining salvation for me through Christ's death on the cross. Help me to keep my part of the bargain by continuing to walk in faith and receiving the rich, bountiful rest you have promised by following your Son. Amen.

EVENING

On My Side

The LORD is on my side; I will not fear.
What can man do to me?
PSALM 118:6 ESV

No matter what happens, we can always be assured that God loves us *with all His heart*, and He will never leave us. He's rooting for us. He's on our side.

Dear Father, thank You for loving me.
Thank You for always being on my side.

Morning

Godly Beauty

Like a gold ring in a pig's snout is a
beautiful woman who shows no discretion.
Proverbs 11:22 NIV

As a woman, no matter your shape or size, your height or hair color, you are *beautiful*. Beauty is in the heart first. It shines forth through attitudes and actions that honor God. This is true beauty.

Lord, when I am tempted to use beauty to attract the world to my body, remind me that a godly woman uses modesty to point the world to You. Amen.

Evening

Oh, Happy Day!

"Until now you have asked nothing in my name.
Ask, and you will receive, that your joy may be full."
John 16:24 ESV

God wants to be the source of your joy. In Him you can find fullness and everything you could need to make you happy. When you love God, your life is filled with so much joy that you don't even chase after those things you once did.

Lord, thank You for providing everything I need to be truly happy. Amen.

DAY
306

Morning

Quiet Hope

It's a good thing to quietly hope, quietly hope for help from God.
Lamentations 3:26 MSG

God calls us to "cease striving" (Psalm 46:10 NASB), so that we can know Him and understand the hope of His calling (Ephesians 1:18). He wants us to quietly hope and wait on God's promises for strength (Isaiah 40:31), for endurance (1 Corinthians 10:13), for peace (Romans 15:13), for salvation (1 Thessalonians 5:8), for eternal life in heaven (Titus 1:2)—for others as well as for ourselves.

Lord, help me to be quiet before You today no matter what is going on around me. I look to the hope I have in Christ Jesus for all I need to do Your will today.

Evening

Natural Beauty

Charm is deceptive, and beauty is fleeting.
Proverbs 31:30 NIV

Imagine what would happen if we spent as much time consciously working on our inner beauty as we did our outer beauty. Wouldn't that be life changing?

Dear Father, sometimes I worry about my appearance. Help me to be content with how You created me, and remind me that my true beauty is inside. Amen.

MORNING

Being of One Mind

Do nothing from selfishness or empty conceit, but with humility of mind regard one another as more important than yourselves.
PHILIPPIANS 2:3 NASB

As Christians we are called to encourage one another in the faith. Many of our brothers and sisters are wounded, both physically and spiritually. Yet they come to Sunday services with a deceptive smile on their faces, their return trip home as lonely as the rest of their week will probably be. Do you care?

Who is my source of strength? Lord, help me encourage others.

EVENING

The Security of God's Love

For I am convinced that neither death nor life, neither angels nor demons, neither the present nor the future, nor any powers, neither height nor depth, nor anything else in all creation, will be able to separate us from the love of God that is in Christ Jesus our Lord.
ROMANS 8:38–39 NIV

When you feel alone, remember that you always have God. He loves you with an everlasting love.

Lord, I am so thankful that nothing can come between us. Remind me on my darkest days that You are always with me. Amen.

MORNING

Masterpiece

*You made all the delicate, inner parts of my body
and knit me together in my mother's womb.*
PSALM 139:13 NLT

He is a big God. Unfathomable. Incomparable. Frankly, words just don't do Him justice. And He made *you*. You were knit together by a one-of-a-kind, amazing God who is absolutely, undeniably, head-over-heels crazy in love with you. Try to wrap your brain around that.

Heavenly Father and Creator, thank You for the amazing gift of life, for my uniqueness and individuality. Help me to use my life as a gift of praise to You. Amen.

EVENING

The Right Friends

*Don't befriend angry people or associate with hot-tempered people,
or you will learn to be like them and endanger your soul.*
PROVERBS 22:24–25 NLT

Sometimes it's hard to find good friends. But remember that God is always with you, and He gives you clear direction so that you can pick the right friends to hang out with.

God, thank You that You are always with me to help me make wise decisions about my friends. Please provide me with friends who want to honor You.

MORNING

Finding Real Rest

And I said, Oh that I had wings like a dove!
for then would I fly away, and be at rest.
PSALM 55:6 KJV

We must jump into God's everlasting arms and dive into His Word. Rest is found in knowing Christ and understanding that through His sacrifice, we are at peace.

As we allow God's peace to fill us, we will find real rest.

Father God, there are many days when I don't have time to sit; remind me that peace comes from knowing You and resting in the work You have done. Amen.

EVENING

What's Love Got to Do with It?

Love is patient, love is kind. It does not envy, it does not boast,
it is not proud. It does not dishonor others, it is not self-seeking,
it is not easily angered, it keeps no record of wrongs.
1 CORINTHIANS 13:4–5 NIV

The world says you only have to love those who love you back. God says there is a more excellent way. God says love everyone. It's not always easy, but how else will the world know that we are His? What's love got to do with it? Just everything.

Dear God, thank You for Your love for me.

DAY
310

Morning

Finding Confidence in Christ

Let us then approach God's throne of grace with confidence,
so that we may receive mercy and find grace to help us in our time of need.
Hebrews 4:16 NIV

When you wonder why in the world God placed you here, remember: we can approach His throne with confidence, finding all we'll ever need to live—and thrive.

Lord, help me to remember that Your arms are open wide,
and I need only to walk into them.

Evening

Ooo-La-La!

Let the king be enthralled by your beauty;
honor him, for he is your lord.
Psalm 45:11 NIV

Today your heavenly Father longs for you to see yourself as the beautiful princess you are. So grab those glass slippers! Let's go to the ball!

God, sometimes I really don't feel pretty at all. I look in the mirror
and don't like the face staring back at me. I'm so glad You think
I'm beautiful! Thank You for seeing my beauty! Amen.

MORNING

How about Some Fun?

A twinkle in the eye means joy in the heart,
and good news makes you feel fit as a fiddle.
PROVERBS 15:30 MSG

God does not want His kids to be worn out and stressed out. We need time to *recreate*—to revive and refresh our bodies and minds. A little relaxation, recreation—and yes—*fun* are essential components of a balanced life. Even Jesus and His disciples found it necessary to get away from the crowds and pressures of ministry to rest.

Lord, help me to find time today for a little
relaxation, recreation, and even fun. Amen.

EVENING

The Path to Take

In all your ways acknowledge Him, and He shall direct your paths.
PROVERBS 3:6 NKJV

We have the awesome privilege today to have God's Word so handy. We can read it in book form, on our computers, even on our iPods or phones! It's truly our guidebook. Filled with stories of triumphs and failures, God's Word is exactly what we need to help us through each day. No matter the obstacle.

Father, I want to know You better,
and I need help in choosing the correct path.

Morning

Babes in Christ

Therefore, putting aside all malice and all deceit and hypocrisy and envy and all slander, like newborn babies.
1 Peter 2:1–2 NASB

As mothers, grandmothers, stepmothers, and aunts, we have a God-ordained call to teach children the Word of God that they might someday enter the kingdom of God.

Lord, lead me to spiritual growth as I read "every word that proceeds out of the mouth of God" (Matthew 4:4 NASB).

Evening

Letting It Go

If we confess our sins, he is faithful and just and will forgive us our sins and purify us from all unrighteousness.
1 John 1:9 NIV

God wants us to honestly admit our sins to Him. He won't erase the consequences because they usually help us remember not to make the same poor decision again; but He also doesn't want us to walk around forever feeling guilty or ashamed. Confess to Him, and let it go. We can't go back in time, but we can *always* have a fresh start with God.

Dear God, thank You for understanding that I will mess up from time to time.

Morning

Inside Out

"Don't you understand either?" he asked.
"Can't you see that the food you put into your body cannot defile you? . . . It is what comes from inside that defiles you."
Mark 7:18, 20 NLT

We can't erase bad thoughts from our minds, but we can crowd them out—by filling our minds with noble, lovely, and true thoughts. "How can a [woman] stay pure? By obeying your word" (Psalm 119:9 NLT).

Lord, search my thoughts, and show me my impurities. Fill me with Your Word.

Evening

Stressful Thoughts

Don't worry about anything; instead, pray about everything.
Tell God what you need, and thank him for all he has done.
Philippians 4:6 NLT

First, you pray! Tell God how you feel and what you need. Then thank Him for how He has always been there for you! The Bible says that doing that will give you a peace in your heart that you can't possibly understand.

Dear God, thank You for giving me answers for all my problems.
When I'm stressed, I will talk to You about it!

Morning

Pace Your Race

Let us strip off every weight that slows us down, especially the sin that so easily trips us up. And let us run with endurance the race God has set before us.
Hebrews 12:1 NLT

The key to finishing the course takes a balance of patience, perseverance, and an unfaltering dependence on our heavenly trainer. God promises an eternal prize for those who persevere, at their own pace, to the end.

Heavenly Father, help me to run this spiritual race balanced with patience, perseverance, and faith. I rely on You to strengthen me on the road of life toward my heavenly reward. Amen.

Evening

Making Time for God's Word

All Scripture is inspired by God and is useful to teach us what is true and to make us realize what is wrong in our lives. It corrects us when we are wrong and teaches us to do what is right.
2 Timothy 3:16 NLT

Start small. Read God's Word five minutes a day and then increase your time as you can. You'll benefit by growing closer to Jesus.

Dear Lord, help me to take time to read the Bible daily, because I want to know You better and learn to do what is right. Amen.

Morning

Desires

The eyes of all look to you, and you give them their food at the proper time. You open your hand and satisfy the desires of every living thing.
Psalm 145:15–16 NIV

We can give to God every desire of our heart, every longing, and every appetite. He can satisfy them. Prayer is the link. As you commune with Him, you will find your desires are either fulfilled or they begin to change to the blessings He wants to give you.

Lord, help me to be open and honest before You with all my yearnings.

Evening

Blankets and Pillows

The goodness of God leadeth thee to repentance.
Romans 2:4 KJV

"Oh, Father," Jemma prayed. "You tried to warn me, but I wouldn't listen. I wanted my own way. I'm so sorry, God. Please. . .please forgive me."

Lord, You are gracious to forgive when I come to You in genuine repentance. Help me to live a life worthy of Your love from this moment forward. Amen.

DAY
316

Morning

Stand Firm and Receive the Crown

Therefore, my beloved brethren whom I long to see,
my joy and crown, in this way stand firm in the Lord, my beloved.
Philippians 4:1 nasb

Speaking like a proud father, Paul refers to these believers at Philippi as his "joy and crown." He brought the Gospel message to them. And then he stood back to watch them grow in their faith. He doesn't want it all to turn to ashes.

Jesus, help me to remember that You surrendered all Your rights
that I might know true freedom. Please show me how to persevere,
make amends, and live in harmony by standing firm in You. Amen.

Evening

You Are So Awesome!

I praise you because of the wonderful way you created me.
Everything you do is marvelous! Of this I have no doubt.
Psalm 139:14 cev

God loves you—*every part* of you. So quit dreaming about being somebody else and celebrate you! Your heavenly Father created you, and He doesn't make mistakes.

God, help me to love myself the way You love me. Amen.

Morning

Stand in the Gap

"I looked for someone among them who would build up the wall and stand before me in the gap on behalf of the land so I would not have to destroy it, but I found no one."
Ezekiel 22:30 NIV

Take time right when you receive a request to talk to the Lord on the requester's behalf. Be the bridge that carries that person through the valley of darkness back to the mountaintop of joy.

Heavenly Father, help me to have a heart of compassion for those I know and even for those I don't know who need Your comfort and love.

Evening

Your Inner Umpire

Let the peace of Christ rule in your hearts.
Colossians 3:15 NIV

Let peace rule in your heart just like an umpire rules a baseball game. Let peace have its way. When peace shows you the way to go, don't ignore it. You'll never be sorry—and you'll stay out of trouble.

Dear Jesus, sometimes it's hard to know what is right and what is wrong. Help me to know Your Word and listen to my inner umpire of peace so that I can be kept from harm. Amen.

DAY
318

MORNING

Ladies in Waiting

I will wait for the LORD. . . .
I will put my trust in him.
ISAIAH 8:17 NIV

Like Isaiah, we need to learn the art of waiting on God. He will come through every time—but in *His* time, not ours. It is when we learn to wait on Him that we will find joy, peace, and patience through the struggle.

Father, You know what I need, so I will wait. Help me be patient, knowing that You control my situation and that all good things come in Your time.

EVENING

Beautifully Designed

"The Spirit of God has made me,
and the breath of the Almighty gives me life."
JOB 33:4 ESV

Do you ever wonder why God loves you so much? You don't have to wonder anymore. God loves You because He made You. He took special time and care to form each feature.

Dear Father, thank You for taking such special care in making me. I know that I am beautifully designed. Thank You for loving me so much.

Morning

God's Precious Promises

His divine power has granted to us everything pertaining to life and godliness, through the true knowledge of Him who called us by His own glory and excellence.
2 Peter 1:3 NASB

Peter reminds us that Jesus Christ is the Savior. "Therefore, brethren, be all the more diligent to make certain about His calling and choosing you; for as long as you practice these things, you will never stumble; for in this way the entrance into the eternal kingdom of our Lord and Savior Jesus Christ will be abundantly supplied to you" (2 Peter 1:10–11 NASB).

God, You promised me a Savior and You sent Jesus. Hallelujah!

Evening

Something Special

And we know that in all things God works for the good of those who love him, who have been called according to his purpose.
Romans 8:28 NIV

Rest assured that God has not forgotten you. Your future may seem cloudy and unpromising now, but God has handcrafted a specific and wonderful plan just for you. He doesn't want you to compare yourself to anyone else, because He created you to be a unique individual.

God, please help me not to compare myself to others.

MORNING

A Godly Guest List

"But when you give a banquet, invite the poor, the crippled, the lame, the blind, and you will be blessed. Although they cannot repay you, you will be repaid at the resurrection of the righteous."
LUKE 14:13–14 NIV

There is certainly reward in heaven for believers who demonstrate kindness. The reward on earth is sweet as well. It may even provide you with an unexpected new friend.

Father, remind me to reach out to others and to be a friend to all types of people. Amen.

EVENING

My Way. . .or Your Way?

We can make our plans, but the LORD *determines our steps.*
PROVERBS 16:9 NLT

It's nice to know the Creator guides us all through our lives—reminding us of His wonderful plan. His way is the best way to find your dreams; after all, He planted them in your heart in the first place.

God, I thank You for all the plans You designed for me. I want to follow Your path to discover the wonderful blessings You have for my life.

MORNING

When I Think of the Heavens

When I consider your heavens, the work of your fingers, the moon and the stars, which you have set in place, what is mankind that you are mindful of them, human beings that you care for them?
PSALM 8:3–4 NIV

The next time you look up at the heavens, the next time you ooh and aah over a majestic mountain or emerald waves crashing against the shoreline, remember that those things, in all of their splendor, don't even come close to you—God's greatest creation.

Oh Father, You love me, and for that I'm eternally grateful!

EVENING

New Things!

Joshua said to them, "Do not be afraid; do not be discouraged. Be strong and courageous. This is what the LORD will do to all the enemies you are going to fight."
JOSHUA 10:25 NIV

New experiences will bring new friends, brand-new adventures, and many blessings. Reach for the door of opportunity God has provided. You just never know where it might lead.

Lord, give me courage in all my activities. Allow the butterflies in my stomach to settle. Amen.

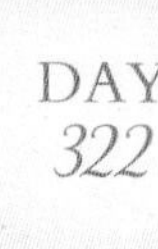

DAY
322

Morning

Sharpening Friendships

Iron sharpeneth iron; so a man
sharpeneth the countenance of his friend.
Proverbs 27:17 KJV

Quality friendships take time. It's beneficial for our health and countenance—and those of our friends—to make that time.

Dear Jesus, I know You are a friend who sticks closer than a sister, yet sometimes I need the comfort of friends I can see and touch. Help me to say no to extra activities so I have time to invest in friends. Amen.

Evening

No One Understands Me Better

You know my sitting down and my rising up;
You understand my thought afar off.
Psalm 139:2 NKJV

Do you ever feel like no one understands you? Not even your family or your friends? Don't they realize they sometimes hurt your feelings or that you are doing the best you can to please them? God knows. He knows you better than anyone else—even better than you know yourself. He knows your heart; He knows your mind.

Dear God, thank You for listening. I feel better already. Amen.

Morning

Hold to God's Truth, Not to Visions

You have died and your life is hidden with Christ in God.
Colossians 3:3 NASB

Paul's message is that Christ in us should cause a change in our lives, for we have been delivered from the "wrath of God" (Colossians 3:6). This metamorphosis should make a visible difference in how we are living our lives, for Christ has set up residence within us.

Let me be cautious of bypassing the Word of God and the Spirit of God to substitute visions of angels for the Gospel.

Evening

I Have Overcome

"These things I have spoken to you, so that in Me you may have peace. In the world you have tribulation, but take courage; I have overcome the world."
John 16:33 NASB

We can memorize and study God's Word. That's what He's given it for! He wants you to meditate on it, beloved. It's your life manual. It shows you who God is, what He likes, how He acts. . . . (See Psalm 119. David knew the importance of God's Word!)

Lord, I need Your strength and courage to overcome these fears. Help me to take up the sword of the Spirit and wield it unceasingly.

DAY 324

Morning

Perfect Prayers

Pray, therefore, like this: Our Father. . .
Out of the depths have I cried to You, O Lord.
MATTHEW 6:9 AMP; PSALM 130:1 AMP

Talk with God while doing dishes, driving the car, folding laundry, eating lunch, or kneeling by your bed. Whenever, wherever, whatever— tell Him. He cares!

Don't allow this day to slip away without talking to your Father. No perfection required.

Father God, what a privilege it is to unburden my heart to You.
Teach me the beauty and simplicity of simply sharing my day with You.

Evening

Make a Wish

For in this hope we were saved. Now hope that is seen is not hope.
For who hopes for what he sees? But if we hope for what
we do not see, we wait for it with patience.
ROMANS 8:24–25 ESV

When we trust that God will do good for us and we surrender our needs to Him, we are trusting in His promises.

Dear Lord, I trust in Your unfailing
Word and surrender my needs to You.

MORNING

The Dream Maker

"No eye has seen, no ear has heard, and no mind has imagined what God has prepared for those who love him."
1 CORINTHIANS 2:9 NLT

God knows the dreams He has placed inside of you. He created you and knows what you can do—even better than you know yourself. Maintain your focus—not on the dream but on the Dream Maker—and together you will achieve your dreams.

God, thank You for putting dreams in my heart. I refuse to quit. I'm looking to You to show me how to reach my dreams. Amen.

EVENING

You Want Me to Love Whom?

"As the Father has loved me, so have I loved you. . . . If you keep my commands, you will remain in my love. . . . I have told you this so that my joy may be in you and that your joy may be complete. My command is this: Love each other as I have loved you."
JOHN 15:9–12 NIV

Jesus makes it pretty clear that loving others isn't an option. He has commanded us to love everyone, even our enemies. Love makes all the difference.

Dear God, thank You for Your love for me.

DAY
326

MORNING

Barriers

So, as those who have been chosen of God, holy and beloved,
put on a heart of compassion, kindness, humility, gentleness and patience;
bearing with one another. . .just as the Lord forgave you, so also should you.
COLOSSIANS 3:12–13 NASB

To say we love Christ and yet maintain deeply rooted prejudices against others is inconsistent with everything He taught. For Christ came to reconcile all peoples to Himself, not separate us into factions.

Lord, let the true peace of Christmas, which is Christ,
be found in my heart as I am obedient to Your command to
love one another, just as You have loved me (John 13:34).

EVENING

My Eternal Shepherd

"My sheep hear My voice, and I know them, and they follow Me.
And I give them eternal life, and they shall never perish;
neither shall anyone snatch them out of My hand."
JOHN 10:27–28 NKJV

Christ has offered you eternal life. The price? Free. He paid it by dying on the cross for your sins. He sacrificed Himself so that you could have the chance to spend eternity with Him.

God, thank You so much for giving me eternal life. Thank You that
You know me, You love me, and nothing can take me from You.

MORNING

A Heavenly Party

"I tell you that in the same way there will be more rejoicing in heaven over one sinner who repents than over ninety-nine righteous persons who do not need to repent."
LUKE 15:7 NIV

If you haven't repented yet, take that step in your faith—don't wait! Heaven's party planners are eager to get your celebration started.

Father, I am so grateful that You rejoice in new Christians. Strengthen my desire to reach the lost while I am here on earth.

EVENING

The Ultimate Superhero

Keep your lives free from the love of money and be content with what you have, because God has said, "Never will I leave you; never will I forsake you."
HEBREWS 13:5 NIV

God is the only friend who will *never* break a promise. It's not in His nature to do so. He will never fail. He knows how to keep a promise—now in this life and for all eternity.

God, thank You that I can trust You with my life in the big things and in the small—and everything in between. Amen.

DAY
328

Morning

Guarding against Compromise

Joyful are those who obey his laws and search for him with all their hearts. They do not compromise with evil, and they walk only in his paths.
Psalm 119:2–3 NLT

We must continually be on guard against making small compromises. These things generally happen gradually—often with one compromise at a time. Many small compromises can lead to devastation. Be on guard and live wisely.

Father, help me to stay connected to You continually. Help me to stay on the wise path and to guard myself against compromise. Amen.

Evening

Kindness Matters

Get rid of all bitterness, rage, anger, harsh words, and slander, as well as all types of evil behavior. Instead, be kind to each other, tenderhearted, forgiving one another, just as God through Christ has forgiven you.
Ephesians 4:31–32 NLT

Use your words for good and not harm.

Dear God, I see how important kindness is to You. Please forgive me for the times when I've acted on my anger instead of being kind.

Morning

Choosing Wisely

Our mouths were filled with laughter.
Psalm 126:2 NIV

We women often plan perfect family events, only to find out how imperfectly things can turn out. Our reactions to these surprise glitches can make or break the event for everyone present. Mom's foul mood sucks the joy from the room. Next time something goes wrong, remember not to take it too seriously.

Lord, give us an extra dollop of grace and peace to laugh about unexpected dilemmas that pop up. And to remember that our reaction is a choice. Amen.

Evening

Understood. . .or Misunderstood?

O Lord, You have looked through me and have known me.
You know when I sit down and when I get up.
You understand my thoughts from far away.
Psalm 139:1–2 NLV

God knows what you're going to say—and why. That's because He can see inside your heart and knows why you're feeling the way you do about things. Not only does He see, but He also truly understands.

Lord, I'm so glad You understand what I think and say.

DAY
330

Morning

The Father Has Bestowed a Great Love

*See how great a love the Father has bestowed on us,
that we would be called children of God; and such we are.*
1 John 3:1 NASB

Have you ever looked into the mirror and thought, *I wish I had a new body*? Well, Christ has one reserved for you in heaven. This body is imperishable, undefiled, and will not fade away (1 Peter 1:3–4).

Lord, as I prepare to celebrate Your birth, the greatest gift I can lay beside the manger is an act of my will that makes me Your child. Yes, I have been born again.

Evening

Inner Beauty

*Your beauty should not come from outward adornment,
such as elaborate hairstyles and the wearing of gold jewelry or fine clothes.*
1 Peter 3:3 NIV

Consider how much time you spend each day on your outward appearance. Now challenge yourself to spend at least that much time in God's Word and prayer. A kind and loving spirit is what your heavenly Father longs to find in you.

God, help me to remember that outward beauty fades but what's on the inside endures forever. Find me beautiful on the inside. Amen.

Morning

Available 24-7

I call on you, my God, for you will answer me;
turn your ear to me and hear my prayer.
Psalm 17:6 NIV

God is always available. He can be reached at any hour of the day or night and every day of the year—including weekends and holidays! When we pray, we don't have to worry about disconnections, hang-ups, or poor reception.

Dear Lord, thank You for always being there for me. Whether I am on a mountaintop and just want to praise Your name or I am in need of Your comfort and encouragement, I can count on You. Amen.

Evening

Enemies

"Love your enemies! Do good to them. Lend to them without expecting to be repaid. Then your reward from heaven will be very great, and you will truly be acting as children of the Most High, for he is kind to those who are unthankful and wicked."
Luke 6:35 NLT

Always be kind, and always be yourself. Treat others the way you want them to treat you. That's what everyone will remember.

Dear Jesus, help me to be a good example and to be kind even when others are not.

DAY
332

Morning

Amnon and Tamar

And Tamar lived in her brother Absalom's house, a desolate woman.
2 Samuel 13:20 NIV

No matter how dark your circumstances, God can redeem them. He can weave your pain into the tapestry of your life and provide hope, help, and healing. You can begin by speaking of the pain then refusing to carry it. Open your heart to God today and receive the gift of healing.

Father, thank You for offering me hope and healing. Help me to let go of the pain of my past so that it does not define me. Redeem it for Your glory. Amen.

Evening

White Noise

"For God so loved the world, that he gave his only Son, that whoever believes in him should not perish but have eternal life."
John 3:16 ESV

Where can you go to get good advice and answers about the things of God? Make sure that, even in the midst of all the noise around you, you're listening carefully for God's voice through the chaos. He will make Himself known to you if you listen closely.

Dear God, please help me hear You through all the noise in my life.

MORNING

Treasure Vault

"For where your treasure is, there your heart will be also."
LUKE 12:34 NIV

Are you gathering earthly treasures or eternal ones? Those on earth won't last. Sending treasures before you to heaven is the wisest thing you can do. Worldly goods fade, but not those in Jesus' treasure vaults.

Lord, help me send treasures ahead of me into eternity instead of grabbing all the earthly items I can get. Amen.

EVENING

Love Letter

So have I loved you.
JOHN 15:9 KJV

My darling,

I want you to trust Me. To believe in Me. Oh, if you will only love Me as I love you, then you can ask Me for anything and I will give it to you. For you are My darling, and My most precious gift is yours.

Will you accept My love?

I shall wait for your answer.

Eternally yours,
God

Dear God, I want to know more about You. As I read Your Word, the Bible, teach me how to love You as You love me. Amen.

DAY
334

Morning

Christmas Joy

And we have seen and testify and proclaim to you the eternal life, which was with the Father and was manifested to us.
1 John 1:2 NASB

Consider today what printed message you will send to loved ones this Christmas. . .a message of hope about Christ the Savior, or a scene in which He is nowhere to be found?

Dear Lord, thank You for the knowledge that Jesus is still the "reason for the season."

Evening

The Green-Eyed Monster

Love is kind and patient, never jealous, boastful, proud, or rude.
1 Corinthians 13:4–5 CEV

Instead of flaws, focus on your positive traits. You are unique! God made you special. You have wonderful talents and strengths. So the next time that green-eyed monster rears its ugly head, turn your head upward and thank God for making you—you!

God, I admit that I am jealous sometimes. Please help me to stop feeling jealous and just focus on being the best version of me. Amen.

Morning

Job's Suffering

Job. . .was blameless, upright,
fearing God and turning away from evil.
Job 1:1 NASB

Job's life became an unwelcome ride on a trolley called tragedy. In one day he lost all his children and his house, servants, and livestock. And through all of this Job refused to sin or blame God.

Lord, as a Christian, lead me so that I do not expect You to be my "celestial Santa Claus." Lead me so I continue to follow, no matter the circumstances.

Evening

Living Forever

I write these things to you who believe in the name of the
Son of God so that you may know that you have eternal life.
1 John 5:13 NIV

Our bodies will die, but our spirits—the part of us that makes us who we are—will live forever in heaven with Jesus and with all those who also believe in Him.

Dear Father, I believe Jesus is Your Son and that He
died in my place as punishment for my sins. Thank You
for sending Him, and thank You for eternal life. Amen.

DAY
336

Morning

Password, Please

And if we are [His] children, then we are [His] heirs also:
heirs of God and fellow heirs with Christ [sharing His inheritance with Him].
Romans 8:17 AMP

Do you have your password, ready to swing open the gates of heaven? It's *Jesus*. Jesus, *period*. No other name is needed, no other combination. You can take that to the bank.

Dear heavenly Father, today I choose to follow You. I give You my life, my all. Teach me Your ways and guard my heart.

Evening

The Best Secret Keeper

Blessed be the God and Father of our Lord Jesus Christ,
the Father of mercies and God of all comfort.
2 Corinthians 1:3 NKJV

Find a quiet, private place where you can tell the Lord what's going on. Hold nothing back. Share it all. He's the best secret keeper there is! Soon you'll experience a release from your burdens as you give them away to Him. He'll show you how to move forward and will comfort you as you go.

Dear God, I know I can depend on You to keep my secrets and trust You to help me find my way. Amen.

Morning

Ordinary Transformed

Now when the Sabbath was past, Mary Magdalene, Mary the mother of James, and Salome bought spices, that they might come and anoint Him.
Mark 16:1 NKJV

There is spiritual value in the monotonous tasks essential to our lives. Often, it's in these times that we are surprised by the Lord, just as the women at His tomb were. As we engage our bodies in work, our minds are free to feel His presence and sense His leading.

Lord, help me to look and listen for You during the ordinary moments of my daily work.

Evening

The Bubble

Don't bother your head with braggarts or wish you could succeed like the wicked. In no time they'll shrivel like grass clippings and wilt like cut flowers in the sun.
Psalm 37:1–2 MSG

Try and get your mind out of the bubble. And pray about that! Think of ways to help other people, get out of your comfort zone, and experience something out of the ordinary!

Dear God, please help me to see outside "the bubble" and not worry so much about the tough seasons in my life that won't last very long.

DAY
338

Morning

Late-Night Counseling

I will praise the Lord*, who counsels me;*
even at night my heart instructs me.
Psalm 16:7 niv

How encouraging to know that God longs to counsel us—to advise. And He's fully aware that nighttime is hard. So, instead of fretting when you climb into bed, spend that time with Him. Meet with Him and expect to receive His counsel.

Father, I trust Your counsel. Speak to me in the night. Instruct my heart.

Evening

Send Your Gorillas Running

Finally, brothers and sisters, whatever is true, whatever is noble,
whatever is right, whatever is pure, whatever is lovely, whatever is admirable—
if anything is excellent or praiseworthy—think about such things.
Philippians 4:8 niv

If you want to be strong to live the way God wants, focus your mind on true thoughts from the Bible such as Philippians 4:13, which says, "I can do all this through him who gives me strength" (niv).

Lord, thank You that You give me strength when I focus on Your truth.
Always help me to fill my mind with Your thoughts. Amen.

Morning

Grace versus the Law

I am amazed that you are so quickly deserting Him who called you by the grace of Christ, for a different gospel; which is really not another; only there are some who are disturbing you and want to distort the gospel of Christ.
Galatians 1:6–7 NASB

Jewish believers were transitioning from the Law, filled with regulations, and beginning to follow the Gospel of grace. However, they easily fell into the trap of "desiring their old robes back."

Paul played a central role in the "persecution of the church of God beyond measure." But seeing Christ face-to-face reduced him to heartfelt repentance. Lord, strengthen my own commitment to You. Show me where I have made my own rules to follow, and give me the courage to replace those self-made laws with Your truth.

Evening

Lots of Friends = Lots of Drama!

*Friends love through all kinds of weather,
and families stick together in all kinds of trouble.*
Proverbs 17:17 MSG

The Bible says that there are "friends" who destroy each other, but a real friend sticks closer than a brother. (And if you're not real fond of your brother right now, you can think of a family member that you are close to. Someone that has your back! That's the idea behind the proverb.)

God, thanks for the friends I have! Help me to be kind and loving to everyone, but to trust my heart to only a few worthy people.

Morning

Creation's Praise

For you created my inmost being;
you knit me together in my mother's womb.
Psalm 139:13 NIV

Before you had a thought or moved a muscle, God was working out a plan for your existence. Whatever His gifts, He designed them just for you, to bring ministry to His hurting world.

Thank You, Lord, for detailing every piece of my body, mind, and spirit. I'm glad nothing that happens to me or in me is a surprise to You. Help me to use all Your gifts for Your glory. Amen.

Evening

Fear Not!

Be strong and of a good courage, fear not, nor be afraid of them: for the Lord thy God, he it is that doth go with thee; he will not fail thee, nor forsake thee.
Deuteronomy 31:6 KJV

On days when you feel afraid of the future. . .of what might happen next . . .of what might be hiding around the corner, remember that God is always with you, always there to watch over you and to lead you.

Dear God, sometimes I am afraid of everything. But I do know that You are there and trust that You will never leave me.

Morning

He Is Coming with the Clouds

Behold, He is coming with the clouds, and every eye will see Him, even those who pierced Him; and all the tribes of the earth will mourn over Him. So it is to be. Amen.
Revelation 1:7 NASB

"We who are alive and remain shall be caught up together with them in the clouds to meet the Lord in the air, and thus we shall always be with the Lord" (1 Thessalonians 4:16–17 NASB). It doesn't get any better than this!

Father, prepare my heart to receive you completely. Thank you, Lord, that my future on earth and beyond is secure in you.

Evening

Obey. . .It's the Safest Way

The promise is this: If you respect your father and mother, you will live a long time and your life will be full of many good things.
Ephesians 6:3 NLV

It's not always easy to obey, is it? So many times we want to have our own way, to do our own thing. If you read today's scripture, you can see that God makes a promise to us when we obey our parents. Even as adults, our lives will be filled with many good things if we just follow the proper direction our parents and our heavenly Father has set for us.

God, it's not always easy to obey! Sometimes I just want to have my own way, to do what I want to do. Help me surrender to Your thoughts and Your ways so I may please You.

Morning

Take Five

The Lord *God formed man of the dust of the ground,*
and breathed into his nostrils the breath of life.
Genesis 2:7 NKJV

Pause from whatever you are doing for just a few moments and breathe deeply. Ask God for a sense of calm and clarity of mind to deal properly with your next assignment.

Sometimes the most active thing we can do is rest, even if for only a short time.

Father, help me not to push myself so hard.
Help me to remember to take five and breathe. Amen.

Evening

Go and Sin No More!

And Jesus said, "I do not condemn you, either.
Go. From now on sin no more."
John 8:11 NASB

We're humans—sinners. Nothing we ever do can erase that (Romans 3:23). But there's good news! God forgives us (Colossians 2:13)! He sent Jesus—the pure, sin-*less* Son of God—to die as a living sacrifice for *our* sins. That means we're forgiven. . .we've been set free (Galatians 5:1)!

Lord, help me to walk in Your Spirit and not in sin.

Morning

Smiles Bring Joy

A cheerful look brings joy to the heart; good news makes for good health.
PROVERBS 15:30 NLT

Joy is contagious; spread it around. Smile at someone today. Go ahead and chuckle at that joke. Laugh with someone. Not only will you be blessing another, but also you will be blessed yourself.

Dear Lord, fill me with Your joy today that I may bless others with my smile and laughter and portray Your love to those around me. Amen.

Evening

How Many Times?

Then Peter came up to Him and said, Lord, how many times may my brother sin against me and I forgive him and let it go? [As many as] up to seven times? Jesus answered him, I tell you, not up to seven times, but seventy times seven!
MATTHEW 18:21–22 AMP

Make the decision to forgive, even if you don't really feel like it. God will bless your offer to let go of a grudge. And you'll get lots of grudge-freeing practice. Remember? Seventy times seven!

Dear Lord, thank You for forgiving me first! Amen.

DAY
344

Morning

God's Message to the Churches

"But I have this against you, that you have left your first love."
Revelation 2:4 NASB

Throughout history, God's church has suffered persecution. But here is a message of hope to all for whom cruelty is a constant companion: remain faithful, God's reward is at hand.

O Lord, may Your light be the fire in my soul!
May your strength sustain me.

Evening

The Cry of Your Heart

Search me, O God, and know my heart; test me and know my anxious thoughts. Point out anything in me that offends you, and lead me along the path of everlasting life.
Psalm 139:23–24 NLT

God's grace is bigger than your sin. And if you really have a desire in your heart to make Him proud, you can pray Psalm 139:23–24. God will always honor that prayer. He'll send the Holy Spirit to nudge you and let you know when something isn't right.

Dear God, keep my feet on the path of everlasting life,
and help me to honor You with my life daily. Amen.

Morning

Jesus as Our Mediator

"If only there were someone to mediate between us. . .
so that his terror would frighten me no more."
Job 9:33–34 NIV

Today, instead of looking at your circumstances, lift your head and look to Jesus. He wants to spare you the terror you are experiencing. When you surrender your situation to Him, He will comfort you with His presence.

Lord, thank You for sending Jesus to be the bridge between us.
Help me to turn to Him—and not run away—in times of fear and doubt.

Evening

Finish Strong!

Let us run with perseverance the race marked out for us,
fixing our eyes on Jesus, the pioneer and perfecter of faith.
Hebrews 12:1–2 NIV

No matter how you're feeling, God wants you to know that He is on your side. He is cheering you on to victory. He has already given you everything you'll ever need to run your race. Just keep your eyes on Him and finish strong.

God, help me to keep my eyes on You and run the race
You have set before me. Help me to finish strong. Amen.

DAY
346

Morning

Behave Yourself!

I will behave myself wisely in a perfect way. O when wilt thou come unto me? I will walk within my house with a perfect heart.
Psalm 101:2 KJV

Because home is a place of comfort and relaxation, it is also the place where we are most likely to misbehave. May God grow us up into mature women, and may we walk accordingly, especially at home.

Father God, how often I fail at home. Make me sensitive to the Spirit so that I will recognize when I am straying from the path of maturity. I'm the adult here; help me to act as one. Amen.

Evening

With Open Arms

Even though I walk through the darkest valley, I will fear no evil, for you are with me; your rod and your staff, they comfort me.
Psalm 23:4 NIV

When you suffer a loss isn't the only time the heavenly Father will wrap you in His loving embrace. He's there to hold your hand when you don't get the promotion you wanted so badly. He's there when you get sick on the night you had special plans. He's there. . .with open arms to comfort you—*always*.

God, thank You for Your comforting arms. Please let me experience Your unconditional love. Amen.

MORNING

Anxiety Check!

Do not be anxious about anything, but in every situation,
by prayer and petition, with thanksgiving,
present your requests to God.
PHILIPPIANS 4:6 NIV

When was the last time you did an anxiety check? Days? Weeks? Months? Chances are, you're due for another. After all, we're instructed not to be anxious about anything. Instead, we're to present our requests to God with thanksgiving in our hearts. We're to turn to Him in prayer so that He can take our burdens. Once they've lifted, it's bye-bye anxiety!

Father, today I hand my anxieties to You.
Thank You that I can present my requests to You.

EVENING

Wow—He Loves Me!

But God demonstrates His own love toward us,
in that while we were still sinners, Christ died for us.
ROMANS 5:8 NKJV

Today, take some time to remember how much He loves you—even though you're a sinner. . .and share that love with someone who may even get on your nerves. You'll be glad you did.

God, help me share Your love with someone else today.

DAY
348

Morning

The Rainbow Surrounding Christ

Behold, a throne was standing in heaven, and One sitting on the throne. . . .
And there was a rainbow around the throne.
Revelation 4:2–3 NASB

God promised Noah that He would never again destroy the world by a flood. As a reminder, God set a rainbow in the clouds (Genesis 9:13–16). Now we see that there is also a rainbow in heaven, as a another promise of things to come.

Lord, thank You that the Babe of Christmas
will one day judge the whole world.

Evening

Hiding Place

You are my hiding place; you will protect me from
trouble and surround me with songs of deliverance.
Psalm 32:7 NIV

The next time you see trouble headed your way, run to God. He'll wrap you in His comforting arms and let you bury your face in His neck. You can know that everything will be okay as long as you use God as your hiding place.

Dear Father, thank You for letting me hide in You
and for delivering me from all kinds of trouble.

Morning

Have You Been with Jesus?

*Now when they saw the boldness of Peter and John,
and perceived that they were uneducated and untrained men,
they marveled. And they realized that they had been with Jesus.*
Acts 4:13 NKJV

When we meditate on scripture and seek the Lord in prayer regularly, we naturally become a little more like Him. Just as slow southern speech points clearly to a particular region on the map, may our lives undeniably reflect that we have been with the Son of God.

Jesus, make me more like You today. Amen.

Evening

All the Way to Your Toes

Finally, be strong in the Lord and in his mighty power.
Ephesians 6:10 NIV

God will give you the strength to stand strong. To be able to walk away when you need to. Or to be able to speak up in love when you know you should. It'll make you feel good inside—not only all the way to your toes, but also all the way to your heart!

*Lord, help me to always know what is right,
and then give me the courage to do it. Amen.*

DAY
350

Morning

Healthy Habits

Since we have these promises, dear friends, let us purify ourselves from everything that contaminates body and spirit, perfecting holiness out of reverence for God.
2 Corinthians 7:1 niv

The investment of exercising, getting enough sleep, and eating properly reaps countless benefits in helping us be more productive, clearheaded, and energetic. God created our earthly bodies to be temples, and we only get one.

Father, thank You for my temple. Help me to care for it to the best of my ability and honor You with healthy habits. Amen.

Evening

Precious and Pleasing

Children, obey your parents in all things: for this is well pleasing unto the Lord.
Colossians 3:20 kjv

Respecting and obeying your parents doesn't end when you move out. Remember that doing so is well pleasing unto the Lord.

Dear God, sometimes it's hard to submit to my parents. Remind me that when I obey them, I'm really obeying You. Amen.

Morning

Difficult People

Do not turn your freedom into an opportunity for the flesh,
but through love serve one another.
Galatians 5:13 NASB

Sometimes, we need to turn our skirmishes with others over to the Lord. Then, by using our weapons—God's Word and a steadfast faith—we need to love and forgive others as God loves and forgives us.

Forgiveness and love seem to be the last thing on my mind. Change my heart, Lord. Help me to love and forgive others as You love and forgive me. Amen.

Evening

Bad News and Good News

Be of good courage, and He shall strengthen your heart,
all you who hope in the Lord.
Psalm 31:24 NKJV

God does allow for things to happen, and yes, it can be scary. But the blessing is that He has called us to be a light for His truth in this dark world, and He will give us the strength we need to carry out that mission.

Lord, help me to be a voice that spreads the truth of Your Word to hurting people. Please give me strength and courage. Amen.

DAY
352

Morning

A Strong Heart

My flesh and my heart may fail,
but God is the strength of my heart and my portion forever.
Psalm 73:26 NIV

Do you ever feel like you have a weak heart? Feel like you're not strong? If so, you're not alone. Twenty-first-century women are told they can "be it all" and "do it all," but it's not true. God never meant for us to be strong every moment of our lives. If we were, we wouldn't need Him.

Father, I feel so weak at times. But I know You are my strength.
Invigorate me with that strength today, Lord.

Evening

Fearfully and Wonderfully Made

I praise you because I am fearfully and wonderfully made;
your works are wonderful, I know that full well. My frame was not hidden
from you when I was made in the secret place, when I was woven
together in the depths of the earth. Your eyes saw my unformed body.
Psalm 139:14–16 NIV

The next time you go somewhere where there are lots of people, look around. Notice how everyone is different. When you do, you'll be amazed by God. How did He make so many different people?

Lord Jesus, thank You so much for making me unique.

Morning

Renewing Our Minds

Do not be conformed to this world, but be transformed by the renewing of your mind, so that you may prove what the will of God is, that which is good and acceptable and perfect.
Romans 12:2 NASB

Paul urges us to resist the ways of this word by renewing our minds with God's truth. Changing the way we think can feel like a battle, and sometimes it is one! The weapons that God provides for us are spiritual. We must become proficient with such an arsenal before such can be effective. So, if the Lord says His Word is a weapon to be used against the enemy, we've got to read it, know it, and follow it.

Lord, I am grateful for the gift that you have given me in your Word; help me to use it wisely.

Evening

Dig In!

Your word is a lamp to my feet and a light to my path.
Psalm 119:105 ESV

After digging through the stories in His Word, you will learn so much! You'll be like flowers, deeply rooted and ready to grow strong and beautiful. So grab your spiritual shovels, and let's start digging!

Lord, thank You for giving me the Bible. It's more than just a book of stories. It's a lamp to light my way. Help me to dig deep so that I can grow strong in You. Amen!

MORNING

The Practice of Praise

Bless the LORD, O my soul; and all that is within me.
PSALM 103:1 KJV

The Bible admonishes us to praise God in every circumstance, saying, "In every thing give thanks: for this is the will of God in Christ Jesus concerning you" (1 Thessalonians 5:18 KJV). To bless the Lord in all things is to receive God's blessings. Begin the practice of praise today!

Heavenly Father, You are worthy of all my praise. I thank and praise You for my current circumstances, knowing that You are at work on my behalf. Amen.

EVENING

A Blob of Goo

But when they measure themselves by one another and compare themselves with one another, they are without understanding.
2 CORINTHIANS 10:12 ESV

Comparing yourself to someone else is kinda like putting peanut butter into a Jell-O mold. You'll always come out looking like a blob of brown goo!

God, please help me not to compare myself to others.
Help me just to be me and to be happy about that!

MORNING

Honor Your Parents

Honour thy father and thy mother: that thy days may be long upon the land which the LORD thy God giveth thee.
EXODUS 20:12 KJV

If your parents are not believers, honor them in every way possible so long as it does not cause you to stumble in your walk with the Lord. We are always called to put the Lord first.

God, help me to honor my parents as You have instructed me to do. Amen.

EVENING

The Finish Line

Do you not know that in a race all the runners run, but only one gets the prize? Run in such a way as to get the prize.
1 CORINTHIANS 9:24 NIV

If we run our race bogged down with sin, temptation, and fear, our race will be slow. But if we allow Jesus to carry those burdens for us, we can run free.

Dear Jesus, please carry my burdens for me so I can run the race free from the weight of this world. I want to cross the finish line and celebrate as I claim my prize. Amen.

DAY
356

Morning

Sharing Our Blessings

Divide your investments among many places,
for you do not know what risks might lie ahead.
Ecclesiastes 11:2 NLT

Many of us have experienced times when God's people have stepped in with a much-needed gift of transportation or food or a car repair. Maybe that's why God tells us to give as much of ourselves and our belongings to as many people as possible. We need the grace of giving *and* receiving.

As we have freely received from God's goodness, may we freely give.

Father, You provide for our needs. Use us to provide for others.

Evening

A Free Do-Over

But God shows his love for us in that while
we were still sinners, Christ died for us.
Romans 5:8 ESV

Just as parents delight in giving their child a gift, so does Jesus delight in giving you a free do-over. And whenever the urge to lie or exclude someone tempts you again, remember that Jesus can give you the strength to avoid the temptation and do the right thing.

Jesus, thank You for giving me unlimited
do-overs whenever I ask for them. Amen.

Morning

The Temple Is Rebuilt

"Let him go up to Jerusalem which is in Judah and rebuild the house of the Lord, the God of Israel; He is the God who is in Jerusalem."
Ezra 1:3 NASB

The Israelites were on the fringe of being brought back to the land God had given them, and now their center of worship was about to be restored!

Lord, my world is filled with uncertainty. But I can be absolutely sure that what You have said will come to pass.

Evening

God Wants Me to Do Right

For it is better, if it is the will of God, to suffer for doing good than for doing evil.
1 Peter 3:17 NKJV

You know what God wants you to do. Ask Him to give you the courage, and then do it.

Dear God, please help me to stand up for what's right and encourage my friends to do the right thing, too. We can find something better to do with our time—something pleasing to You. Please give me the desire in my heart to always do what's right. Amen.

MORNING

Happy Birthday, Jesus!

Joseph also went up from Galilee, from the city of Nazareth, to Judea, to the city of David which is called Bethlehem.
LUKE 2:4 NASB

Joy fills our hearts as we celebrate Christmas. But are we mindful of the sacrifices surrounding this tiny Savior's birth? Christ, the Son of God, willingly left heaven's throne, took on a human body, and grew to manhood so He could die on the cross.

Father, Your Word is all I need today: "Behold, a virgin will be with child and bear a son, and she will call His name Immanuel" (Isaiah 7:14 NASB*).*

EVENING

An Invitation to Rest

Then Jesus said, "Come to me, all of you who are weary and carry heavy burdens, and I will give you rest."
MATTHEW 11:28 NLT

Go to Him and give Him the hard things you're going through. He wants to listen. But it doesn't stop there. He also wants to give you rest. He may not take away the tough times, but He will comfort you as you go through them.

Dear Lord, thank You for caring about the times that I struggle.

Morning

Blessing, Not Blasting

Bless the Lord, O my soul: and all that is within me, bless his holy name.
Psalm 103:1 KJV

Every day God stacks His gifts around us as if it were Christmas. Like children, we can't give Him much. But we can offer all we are to bless His holy name. And that's the present He loves most.

Lord, each day I encounter thousands of opportunities to bless You, the Lord of the universe. Help me seize the day and praise You whenever I can!

Evening

Do You Feel Like You Don't Fit In?

Now you are the body of Christ, and each one of you is a part of it.
1 Corinthians 12:27 NIV

God has a very special plan for you. This is why there will be times when you can't—and shouldn't—do what everyone else is doing. You won't look like them, wear the same clothes, or have the same interests, because God has something special for you to do that they can't do.

Lord Jesus, I am Your amazing creation. Help me to remember this when I feel like I don't fit in. Amen.

Morning

King Forever

You, O God, are my king from ages past,
bringing salvation to the earth.
Psalm 74:12 NLT

God's reign will continue until the day His Son returns to earth, and then on into eternity. We can rely—absolutely depend on—His unchanging nature. Take comfort in the stability of the King—He's our leader now and forever!

Almighty King, You are my Rock. When my world is in turmoil and changes swirl around me, You are my anchor and my center of balance. Thank You for never changing. Amen.

Evening

Fighting through Rough Times

"Do not let your heart be troubled; believe in God, believe also in Me."
John 14:1 NASB

God gave you an amazing gift for the rough times: prayer. He's always here to listen. And He asks you to call out to Him (Matthew 7:7–8). Even if you don't know what to say, His Spirit "intercedes for us with groanings too deep for words" (Romans 8:26 NASB). God knows your tender heart, and He will help you along every step of the way.

Father, thank You for Your everlasting love,
Your always-within-reach comfort, and the wonderful gift of prayer.

Morning

Order in Our Prayers

This is good and acceptable in the sight of God our Savior, who desires all men to be saved and to come to the knowledge of the truth.
1 Timothy 2:3–4 NASB

Prayer isn't some mystical entity to be attained by a few saintly little ladies in the church. Instead, it is an act of worship on the part of the created toward the Creator. Prayer is simply "talking to God" about everything that affects our lives.

Spirit of God, fall afresh on me that I might lift my voice in petition to You.

Evening

Encourage Yourself!

But David encouraged himself in the Lord his God.
1 Samuel 30:6 KJV

No matter how many times you feel like giving up, *don't*! Just follow David's example. Encourage yourself in the Lord, and watch your situation turn around!

God, help me to be quick to encourage myself by thinking about You and Your goodness to me.

DAY
362

Morning

Keeping Christmas

"For there is born to you this day in the city of David a Savior, who is Christ the Lord."
Luke 2:11 NKJV

This year let Christmas stay. As December melts into January and a new year begins, *keep Christmas.* Let the Christ of Christmas make every day a little happier, a little brighter, a little bigger. Make *life* the special occasion, not just December 25.

Father, thank You for the gift of Your only Son, sent that I might have life instead of death. Help me to keep the spirit of Christmas in my heart and celebrate Jesus all year long. Amen.

Evening

You Are Always on His Mind

How precious are your thoughts about me, O God. They cannot be numbered!
Psalm 139:17 NLT

The Bible says that you are fearfully and wonderfully made. God knew you before you were born, and He thinks about you all the time. His love for you will last forever.

Dear God, thank You that I am important to You. I'm thankful that You are always thinking of me. I'm grateful that You love me and created me for a special purpose. Help me always to walk close to You so that I can be all You created me to be. Amen.

MORNING

Going Above and Beyond

Now to him who is able to do immeasurably more than all we ask or imagine, according to his power that is at work within us, to him be glory in the church and in Christ Jesus throughout all generations, for ever and ever!
EPHESIANS 3:20–21 NIV

Praise the Lord! Praise Him in the church and throughout all generations! He's an immeasurable God.

Heavenly Father, it's amazing to realize You have more power in Your little finger than all of mankind has put together. Today I praise You for being a God who goes above and beyond all I could ask or imagine.

EVENING

Hidden in My Heart

Your commands are always with me
and make me wiser than my enemies.
PSALM 119:98 NIV

There always seem to be people who are very difficult to get along with and try our patience. When those people come along, remember to talk to God about it and ask for patience.

Thank You, God, for Your Word. Your Word encourages and gives me commands that will live within me forever and ever. Amen.

DAY 364

MORNING

A New Day

GOD, treat us kindly. You're our only hope. First thing in the morning, be there for us! When things go bad, help us out!
ISAIAH 33:2 MSG

Every day is a new day, a new beginning, a new chance to enjoy our lives—because each day is a new day with God. No matter what happened the day before, we have a fresh start to enjoy a deeper relationship with Him.

Before I get out of bed in the morning, let me say these words and mean them: "This is the day the LORD has made; we will rejoice and be glad in it" (Psalm 118:24 NKJV).

EVENING

True Beauty

"The LORD does not look at the things people look at. People look at the outward appearance, but the LORD looks at the heart."
1 SAMUEL 16:7 NIV

A beautiful person is kind and compassionate. A beautiful person cares about people and shows love to everyone—no matter what. A beautiful person makes others feel important and lets them know how special they are.

Dear Father, thank You for teaching me the true definition of beauty. When You look at my heart, I want You to see a beautiful person.

DAY
365

Morning

Bright Future

Take therefore no thought for the morrow:
for the morrow shall take thought for the things of itself.
MATTHEW 6:34 KJV

Even if you could get your hands on a crystal ball, knowing the future wouldn't prepare you for it. That's why God has chosen not to show you what lies ahead. He wants you to live moment by moment, *trusting Him*!

Dear Father, remind me that no matter what the future holds,
You've got everything under control. Amen.

Evening

Seek and Trust

The LORD is a stronghold for the oppressed, a stronghold in times of trouble.
And those who know your name put their trust in you, for you,
O LORD, have not forsaken those who seek you.
PSALM 9:9–10 ESV

When you have walked with God through life for any amount of time, you experience His absolute faithfulness. This brings trust—a deep knowing—that God is ultimately good and has your best interests in mind.

Lord, thank You for being my own personal stronghold.

Scripture Index

OLD TESTAMENT

NEW TESTAMENT